Mel Bay's First Lessons Blues Guitar

by Mike Christiansen
& Corey Christiansen

1 2 3 4 5 6 7 8 9 0

CD CONTENTS

1. Tuning
2. First Chords #2
3. First Chords #3
4. First Chords #4
5. Ain't No Cure
6. Strum Patterns Exercise
7. Strum Patterns #1
8. Strum Patterns #2
9. Strum Patterns #3
10. Sun Won't Shine
11. Notes on the First String
12. Notes on the Second String
13. Mama's Cookin'
14. No Time To Practice Blues
15. I Got No Money
16. Notes on the Third String
17. Help Yourself
18. Notes on the Fourth String
19. Seven Minus Three
20. Dark Side of a Dream
21. Freezing Point
22. Notes on the Fifth String
23. Double Trouble
24. Notes on the Sixth String
25. Long Road Home
26. Cry, Baby
27. Things Ain't the Same
28. Power Chords #1
29. Power Chords #2
30. Power Chords #3
31. Power Chords #4
32. Solo 1
33. Solo 2
34. Blues E
35. Blues A
36. Summer Blues, Summer Not
37. I Know What You Mean

MEL BAY — It doesn't get any easier.....

© 2001 BY MEL BAY PUBLICATIONS, INC., PACIFIC, MO 63069.
ALL RIGHTS RESERVED. INTERNATIONAL COPYRIGHT SECURED. B.M.I. MADE AND PRINTED IN U.S.A.
No part of this publication may be reproduced in whole or in part, or stored in a retrieval system, or transmitted in any form
or by any means, electronic, mechanical, photocopy, recording, or otherwise, without written permission of the publisher.

Visit us on the Web at www.melbay.com — E-mail us at email@melbay.com

Table of Contents

Introduction 3
Parts of the Guitar 4
Holding Position 5
Tuning 7
Reading the Music Diagrams 8
Music Fundamentals 9
Strum Bars 9
First Chords 10
Blues in the Key of D 11
Blues in the Key of E 12
    Ain't No Cure 12
Strum Patterns 13
    Baby Don't Love Me 15
    Ain't Got a Nickel 15
Building the Blues 16
    Set Me Free 17
Minor Blues 18
    Sun Won't Shine 18
How to Read Standard Notation 19
Standard Notation in First Position 20
Notes on the First String 20
Notes on the Second String 20
    Mama's Cookin' 21
    No Time to Practice Blues 21
    I Got No Money 21
Notes on the Third String 22
Notes on the Fourth String 22
    Seven Minus Three 23
    Dark Side of a Dream 23
    Freezing Point 24
Notes on the Fifth String 25
    Double Trouble 25
Notes on the Sixth String 26
    Long Road Home 26
    Cry, Baby 27
    Things Ain't the Same 27
Power Chords 28
    Add the Sixth 29
Tablature 31
Minor Pentatonic and Blues Scales 32
    Blues E 33
    Blues A 34
Moveable Minor Pentatonic Scale 35
Summer Blues, Summer Not 36
I Know What You Mean 37
Writing Blues Lyrics 38
Writing Your Own Blues Song 39
Common Blues Chords 40

Introduction

This beginning guitar method is unique because the style of music used throughout the entire book is the blues. Using the blues as the vehicle, this method presents the fundamentals of playing guitar. Accompaniment and solo techniques are presented. The book contains sections on strumming, reading standard notation and tablature, power chords, and the scales used in building an improvised solo. Another section in the book is devoted to learning to write original blues lyrics.

This book is written so it can be studied front to back, or by skipping from section to section. For example, one could learn the basic chords and strum patterns, then skip to the section which presents notes on the first two strings. After learning those notes, one could skip to the section on power chords.

Parts of the Guitar

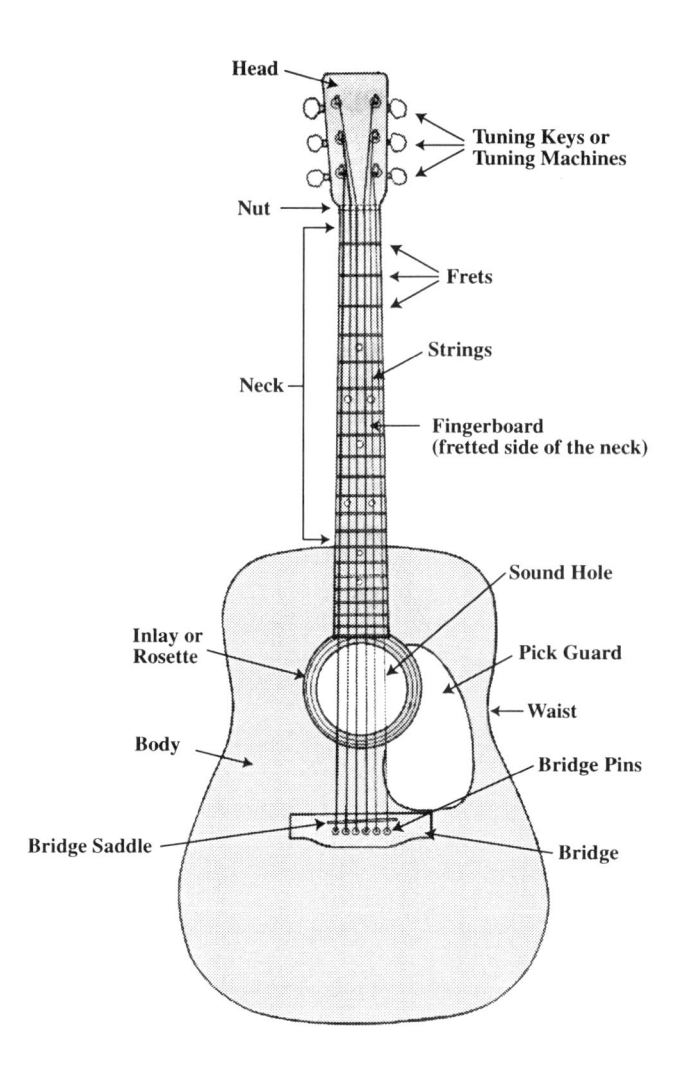

Care of the Guitar

Here are some tips to keep in mind for taking care of the guitar:

1) Make sure the correct type of strings are on the guitar. There are basically two types of strings: nylon and steel. Nylon strings are used on the classical guitar and steel strings are used on the steel string acoustic (folk) guitar and electric guitar (unless the electric has an "acoustic" pick-up). Steel strings which are bronze are for the steel string acoustic guitar. Bronze strings do not work well on electric guitars unless the electric has an "acoustic pick-up". Most guitars play best if they are strung with medium or light gauge strings. Note: heavy gauge strings may warp the neck on some guitars.

2) Avoid rapid temperature and/or humidity changes. A rapid change could damage the finish and the wood of the guitar. Do not leave the guitar in a car when the weather is very hot or cold, and try not to leave the guitar next to heater vents or air conditioners. If the climate is extremely dry, a guitar humidifier can be used to prevent the guitar from drying and cracking.

3) Polish the guitar. Polish which is made specifically for guitars can be purchased from a music store. Besides keeping the guitar looking nice, polishing the guitar will help protect the finish and the woods. Be careful not to polish the fingerboard.

4) If the guitar is being shipped or taken on an airplane, always loosen the strings. The strings do not have to be completely loose, but should be loose enough that the tension of the strings pulling on the neck is greatly reduced.

Holding Position

If the guitar is held properly, it will feel comfortable to you. In the **sitting position,** the guitar is held with the waist of the guitar resting on the right leg. The side of the guitar sits flat on the leg with the neck extending to the left. The neck should be tilted upward slightly so the left arm does not rest on the left leg. Both feet should be flat on the floor, although some guitarists prefer to elevate the right leg by using a footstool. The right arm rests on the top of the guitar just beyond the elbow. The right hand should be placed over and to the back (towards the bridge) of the sound hole. Whether using a pick or the fingers, the right-hand fingers should be bent slightly. The right-hand fingers may touch the top of the guitar, but they should not be stationary. They move when stroking the strings.

The left hand should be positioned with the thumb touching the back of the guitar neck. Do not bend the thumb forward. The thumb should be vertical, touching the neck at the knuckle. Do not position the thumb parallel with the neck. The palm of the left hand should not touch the guitar neck. The left wrist may bend *slightly,* but be careful not to exaggerate the bend.

When placing a left-hand finger on the string, "square" the finger and push on the string using the tip of the finger. (The fingernails must be short so the tip of the finger can be used.) The finger should be positioned just behind and touching (when possible) the fret wire. Placing the finger too low in the fret may result in a buzz, and placing the finger on top of the fret wire may cause a muted sound. The left-hand knuckles should run parallel with the guitar neck. This makes it possible to reach higher frets with the left-hand third and fourth fingers without turning the wrist. Again, be careful not to bring the left-hand thumb over the top of the guitar neck, and do not touch the guitar neck with the palm of the hand. When pushing on the string, it is as though the guitar neck and string are being pinched between the thumb and finger.

Push the string firmly enough to get a sound, but don't over push. To determine the correct amount of pressure, touch the string with the left-hand finger and gradually apply pressure. Pick the string over and over. When a clear sound occurs, that's the amount of pressure to use.

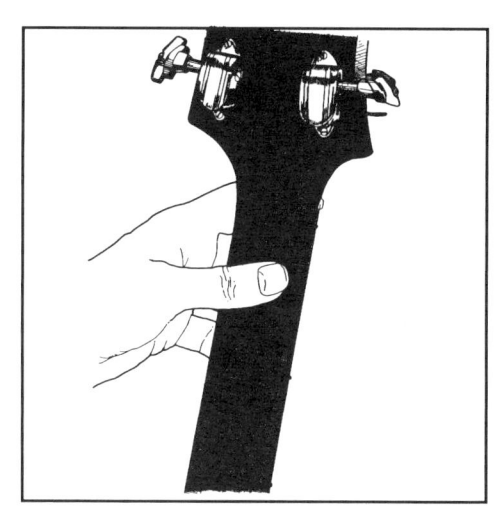

Rest your right-hand thumb on the first (the smallest) string and stroke the open string (open means no left-hand fingers are pushing on the string) downward. Make sure the right-hand wrist moves, and the arm moves slightly from the elbow. The right-hand fingers may touch the top of the guitar, but they should move when the string is played. Try to have a relaxed feeling in the right hand. Go straight down with the thumb when stroking the string. Next, with the right-hand thumb, play the second string open. When playing a string other than the first string, the thumb should go straight down and rest upon (but not play) the next smallest string. In classic guitar playing, this is called a **rest stroke.**

Strumming refers to playing three or more strings so the strings sound simultaneously. To practice the strumming action, rest the right-hand thumb on the fourth string and strum four strings. Using a down stroke, let the right hand fall quickly across the strings so they sound at the same time. The right-hand wrist and arm move with the action.

To hold the pick correctly, first, bend the right-hand index finger. The other fingers of the right hand also bend, but not as much as the index finger.

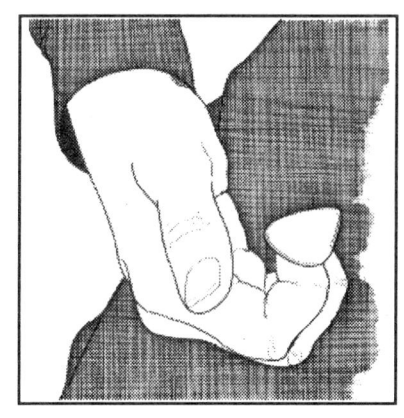

The pick is placed on the end of the index finger with the pointed part of the pick aiming directly at the strings.

The thumb is placed over the pick, covering 2/3 to 3/4 of the pick..

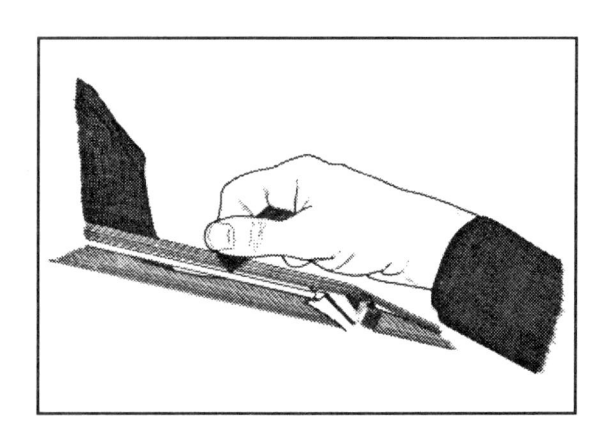

To place the right hand (with the pick) in playing position, rest the pick on the first string. The pick should be tilted upward slightly, rather than at a direct right angle to the string. The pick should stroke the string just over and to the back (towards the bridge) of the sound hole. Pick the first string down. The right-hand wrist should move slightly when the string is played, and the right arm should move slightly from the elbow. When playing strings other than the first, after stroking the string, the pick should rest on the next smallest string. This action is a type of **rest stroke,** which is commonly used in fingerstyle playing, and will generate a richer and fuller tone than picking with an outward motion will. Try playing each of the strings using this type of motion.

To get the feel of strumming with the pick, rest the pick on the fourth string and strum four strings down. Be sure to have a relaxed right hand. Move the wrist and arm slightly when doing the strumming. When picking a single string, or strumming, upward, the pick is tilted down slightly so the pick will glide across the strings, rather than "bite" or snag them.

Tuning

There are several methods which can be used to tune the guitar. One way to tune the guitar is to tune it to itself. You can tune the first string of the guitar to a piano, pitch pipe, tuning fork, or some other instrument, and then match the strings to each other. To do this, use the following steps:

▶ 1. Tune the first open string to an E note. (Remember, open means that no left-hand fingers are pushing on the string.) You can use a piano, pitch pipe, tuning fork, or another instrument. If you use a tuning fork, use an "E" tuning fork. Hold the fork at the bass and tap the fork on your knee, or another object, to get the fork to vibrate. Then, touch the bass of the fork near the bottom of the bridge of the guitar. The pitch which will sound is the pitch the first string should have when the string is played open.

▶ 2. After the first string is tuned, place a left-hand finger on the second string in the fifth fret. Play the first and second strings together. They should be the same pitch. If not, adjust the second string to match the first.

▶ 3. Place a finger on the third string in the fourth fret. The third string should now sound the same as the second string open. If not, adjust the third string.

▶ 4. Place a finger on the fourth string in the fifth fret. The fourth string, fifth fret should sound the same as the third string open.

▶ 5. Place a finger on the fifth string, fifth fret. This should sound the same as the fourth string open.

▶ 6. Place a finger on the sixth string, fifth fret. The sixth string, fifth fret should sound the same as the fifth string, open.

The diagram below shows where the fingers are placed to tune the guitar to itself.

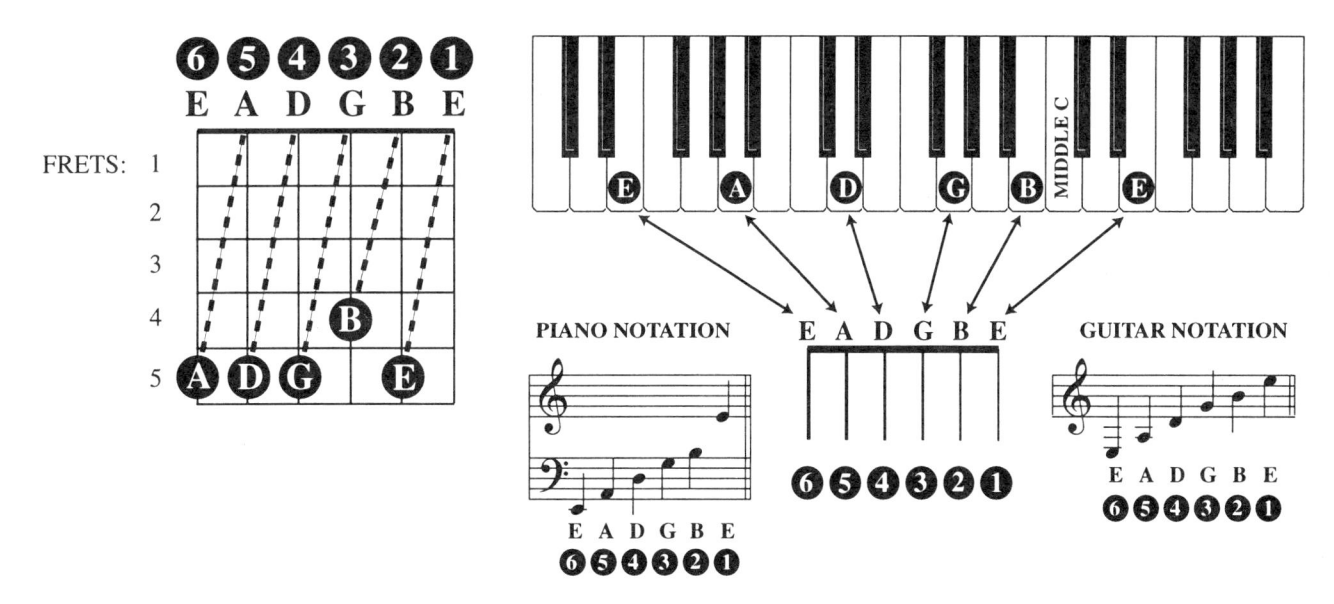

Another common method of tuning is the use of an **electronic tuner**. Tuners utilize lights (LEDs) or Vu meters to indicate if a string is sharp or flat. Tuners have built in microphones or electric guitars can be plugged in directly. Follow the instructions provided with the tuner. If the tuner does not respond to playing a string, make sure you are playing the correct string and, if it is adjustable, the tuner is set for that particular string. Sometimes on the lower notes, the tuner won't function properly. If this happens, try playing the harmonic on the twelfth fret of the string. To do this, place a left-hand finger on the string over the twelfth fret-wire. Touch (do not push) the string very lightly. Pick the string. A note should be heard which will have a "chime" effect. This is a harmonic. It will ring longer if the left-hand finger is moved away from the string soon after it is picked. The electronic tuner will most likely respond to this note.

Reading the Music Diagrams

The music in this book will be written using chord diagrams, tablature and standard notation.

Chord diagrams will be used to illustrate chords and scales, With the chord diagrams, the vertical lines represent the strings on the guitar, with the first string being on the right. The horizontal lines represent frets, with the first fret being on the top. Dots, or numbers, on the lines show the placement of left-hand fingers. The numbers on, or next to the dots indicate which left-hand finger to use. A diamond may be used to indicate the placement of the root of the chord or scale. **Root** refers to a note which has the same letter name as the chord or scale.

A zero above a string indicates the string is to be played open (no left-hand fingers are pushing on the string). An "X" above a string indicates that string is not to be played, or that the string is to be muted by tilting one of the left-hand fingers and touching the string lightly.

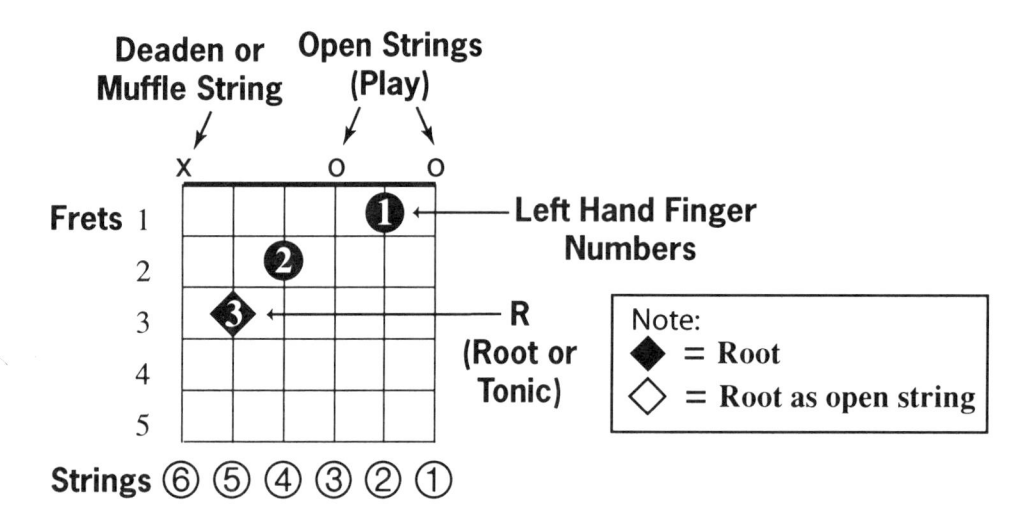

Left-Hand Fingers

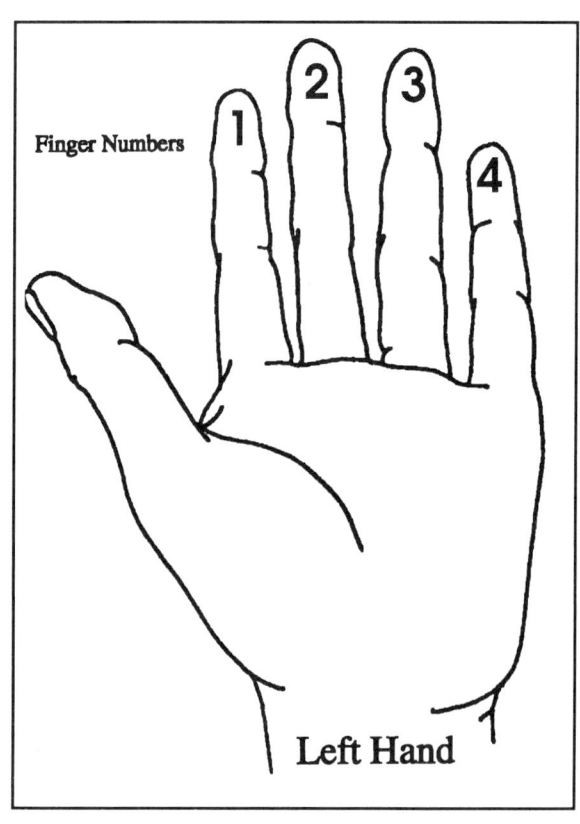

Music Fundamentals

The five lines and four spaces in music is called a **staff**. At the beginning of each line, a treble clef, or G clef, is written on the staff. The treble clef will be discussed later. The staff is divided into sections with **bar lines**. The sections between the bar lines are called **measures**. Inside each measure there are **beats**. Beats are the pulse of the music or measurements of time. The number of beats in each measure can be determined by looking at the **time signature**. The time signature is the fraction which appears at the beginning of the music.

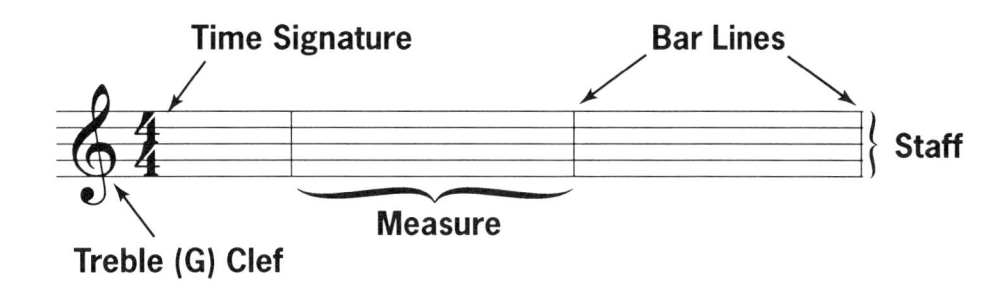

The top number in the time signature indicates the number of beats in each measure. The bottom number in the time signature will be discussed later in the book. If "C" is written, the piece is in 4/4. C stands for **common time**.

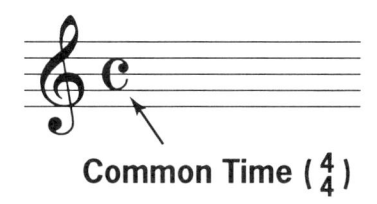

Strum Bars

A **chord** is when three or more strings are played at the same time. Often, when playing chords, the strings are strummed. For the exercises and songs in this book, the chords will be strummed with a pick. For the holding position of the pick, see page 6. When strumming, the right-hand wrist rotates slightly, and the arm moves from the elbow as the pick moves across the strings. When strumming the strings down, be sure to strum straight down. Do not strum outward. Written below are several strum bar signs. Each is a down strum, but the length of the strum varies. The time value of each strum is written to the side. This mark, ⊓, written above the strum bar, indicates a downstroke. If the strum gets more than one beat, strum the strings on the first beat, and allow them to ring for the additional beats. Practice playing each strum bar several times while strumming all six strings open. **Open** means that <u>no</u> left-hand fingers are pushing on the strings.

Practice the following rhythm exercise strumming all six strings open. Strumming the strings open may seem a bit strange at first, but the object is to play the correct rhythm and not be concerned with holding chords. Tap your foot on the beat (four times in each measure). The pick should be used to do the strum.

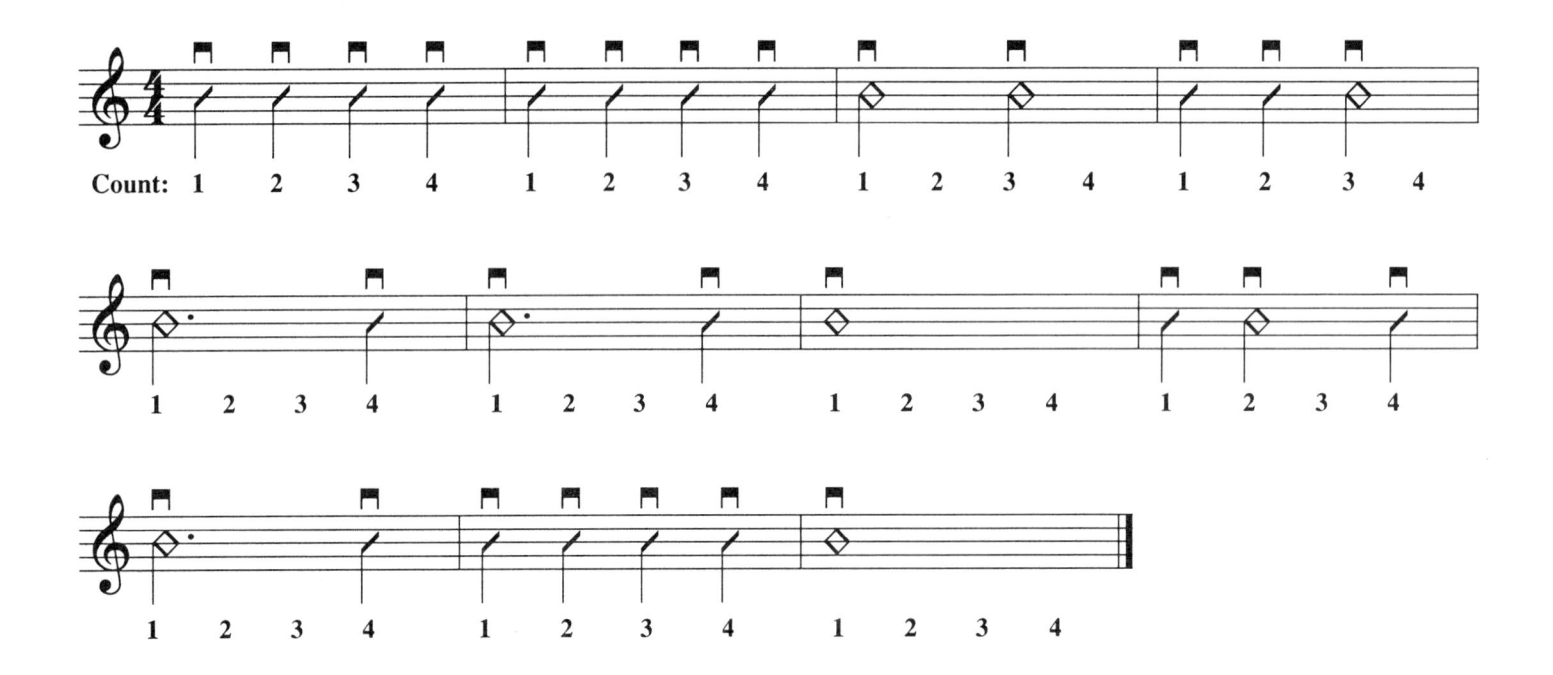

First Chords

The three basic chords used to play the blues in the key of A are: A7, D7, and E7. These three chords are drawn below. See page 8 for the explanation on how to read the chord diagrams. Practice strumming each chord down several times, and then practice changing from one chord to another. Mix the three chords in any order. Be careful to strum the correct number of strings on each chord.

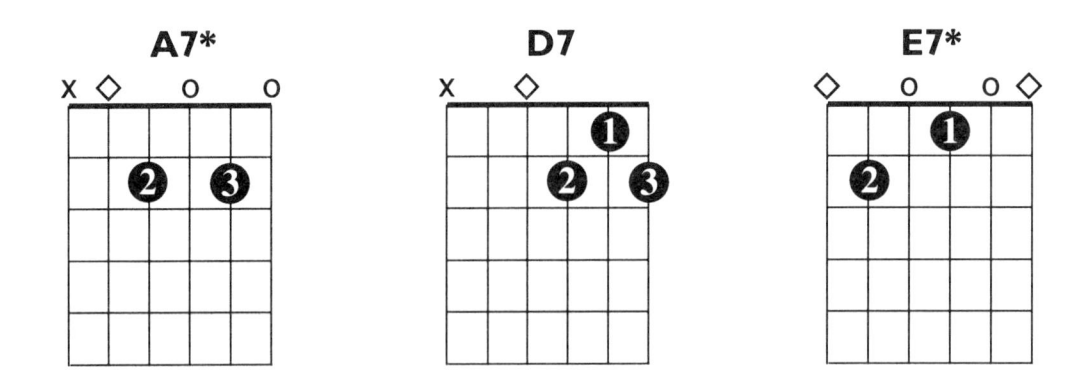

A "progression" is a series of chords. The following exercises is a 12-bar blues progression. 12-bar means the progression is 12 measures long. The formula for building the 12-bar blues progression will be presented later in this book. Because the following exercise in is 4/4 time, strum down four times in each measure. The chord to be strummed is written above the measure. If a chord is not written above the measure, play the chord which was written above the previous measure.

See page 40 for the optional fingerings of the A7 and E7 chords

10

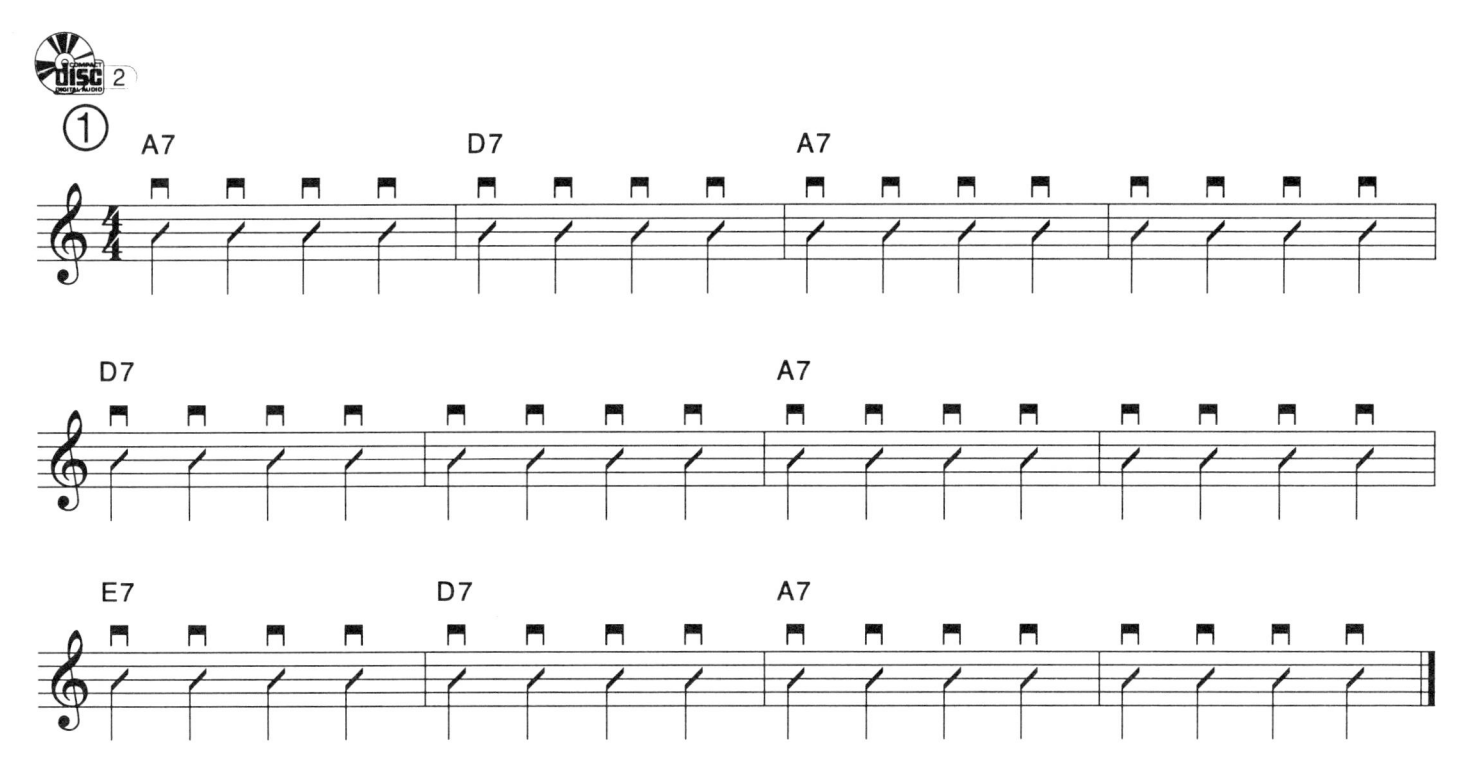

Blues in the Key of D

The chords used to play the blues in the key of D are: D7, G7, and A7. The D7 and A7 chords were used to play the blues in the key of A. The G7 chord is drawn below.

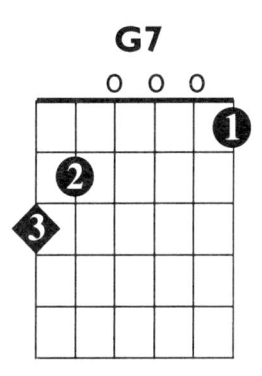

Practice strumming the following blues progression in the key of D. Strum down four times in each measure.

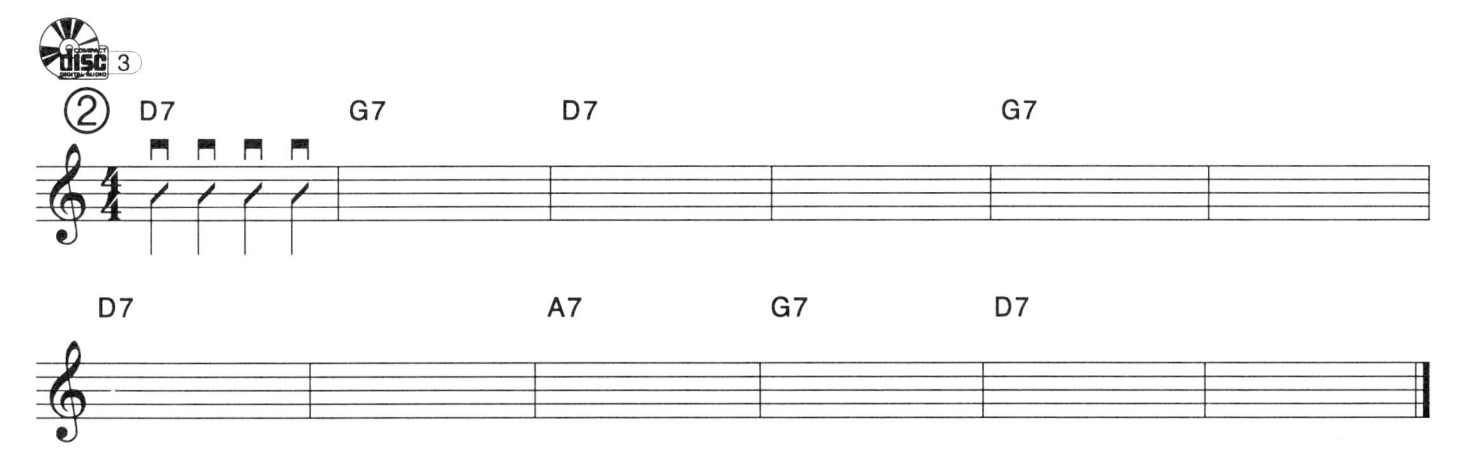

Blues in the Key of E

The chords used to play the blues in the key of E are: E7, A7, and B7. The E7 and A7 chords have been used earlier. The B7 chord is drawn below.

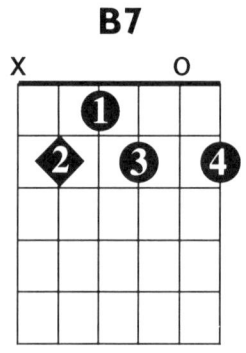

B7

Practice the following blues progression in the key of E. Strum down four times in each measure.

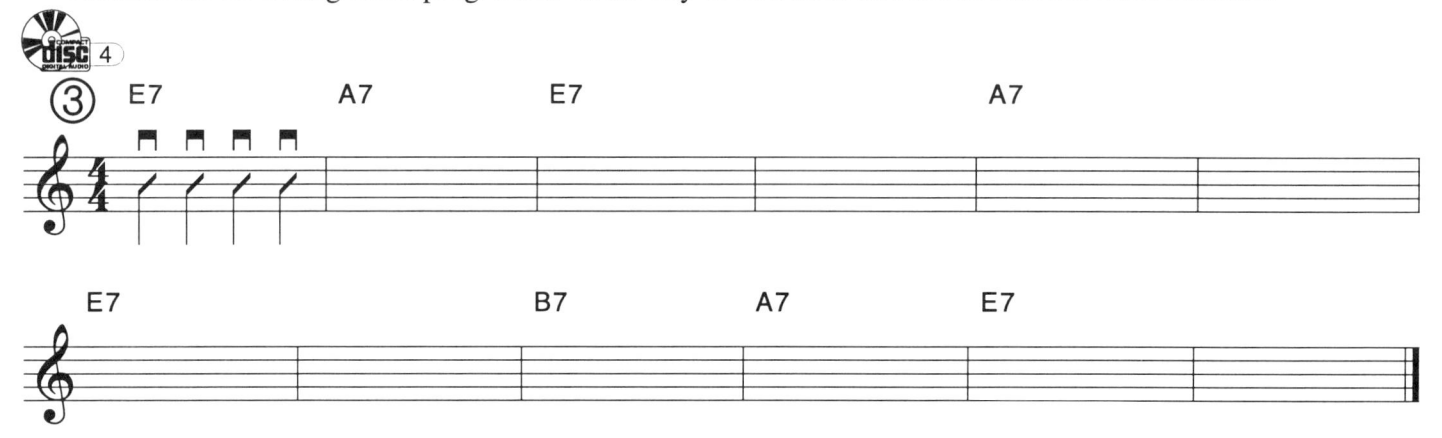

| E7 | A7 | E7 | A7 |

| E7 | B7 | A7 | E7 |

Play the chords to the following song. It is a blues in the key of A. Strum down four times in each measure. Strumming down four times in each measure is a strum pattern which, although simple, is quite commonly used for blues in 4/4. The chords to be strummed are written above the measures. Do not be concerned with the notes. Observe the chords above the measures, the number of measures each chord gets, the time signature, and the lyrics to be sung in each measure. As the notes are learned, it will become easy to play the melody. For now, to learn the melody, have it played on the piano or have someone who can play notes on the guitar play the melody.

Ain't No Cure

A7   D7   A7

I went to the doc-tor   said, "Could you help me please?"

D7   A7

I went to the doc-tor   said, "Could you help me please?"   He said,

E7   D7   A7

"Son there ain't no cure 'cause the blues is your di-sease."

Strum Patterns

A **strum patterns** can be used to create interest to the accompaniment. A strum pattern can consist of a combination of down and up strums. A down-strum is indicated with this sign,⊓, written above the strum bar. The up strum is indicated with this sign,V, written above the strum bar. Regardless of the chord being played, when doing an up-strum, only the first (highest sounding) three or four strings should be strummed. The pick should be used and angled downward slightly when doing the up-strum. When two strums are connected with a beam, they are called eighth note strums. When playing eighth-note strums, there are two notes played in one beat. The first strum bar is a downstroke and is played on the first half of the beat. The up-strum is played on the second half of the beat. The eighth-note strum is the strum equivalent to eighth notes in standard notation. Eighth notes will be presented later in this book. The downstroke is counted as the number of the beat on which it occurs, and the up strum is counted as "and," example:

one and

Very often, eighth-note strums are played using **swing rhythm.** In swing rhythm, rather than the beat being divided into two equal parts, the down-strum gets about two-thirds of the beat and the up-strum gets the remaining one-third of the beat.

If playing with swing rhythm is difficult at first, think of the melody to "Battle Hymn of the Republic." This melody is often sung with swing rhythm. If a piece of music is to be played using swing rhythm, sometimes this, ♫ = ♩♪ will be written at the beginning of the music. Practice the following exercise playing the down and up strums evenly. Then, repeat the exercise using swing rhythm.

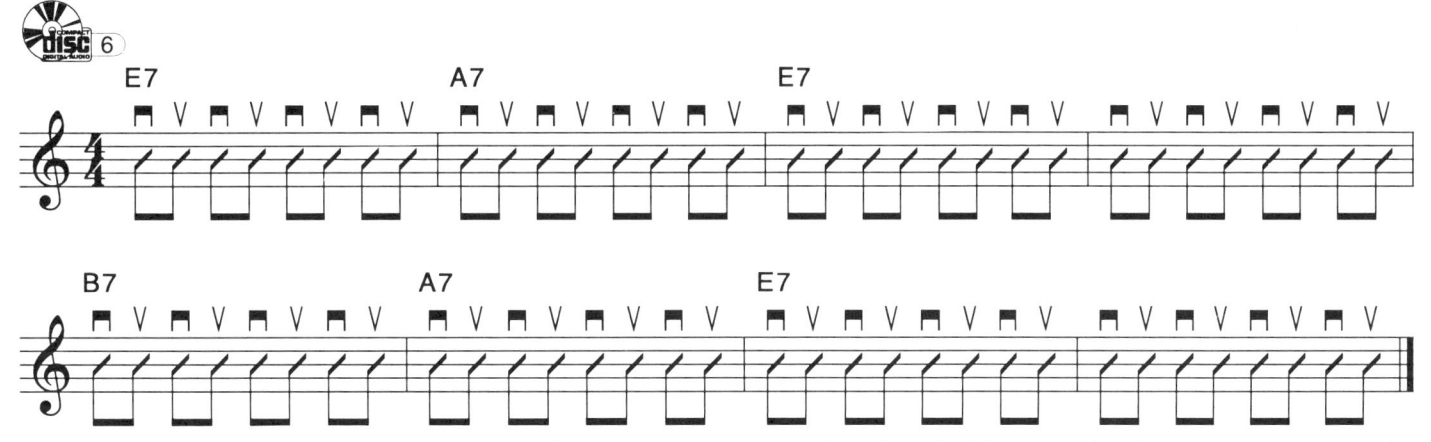

Written below are six strum patterns which are commonly used to play the blues. Each of the strum patterns take one measure of 4/4 to complete and can be used to play any blues song in 4/4. Once a pattern has been selected, play the same pattern in each measure of the piece. It is uncommon to combine patterns.

Practice holding any chord and play each pattern. Be careful to use the correct strum direction and correct rhythm. Tap your foot on each beat and count the rhythms aloud. The patterns are written in order of difficulty. Master one pattern before moving to the next.

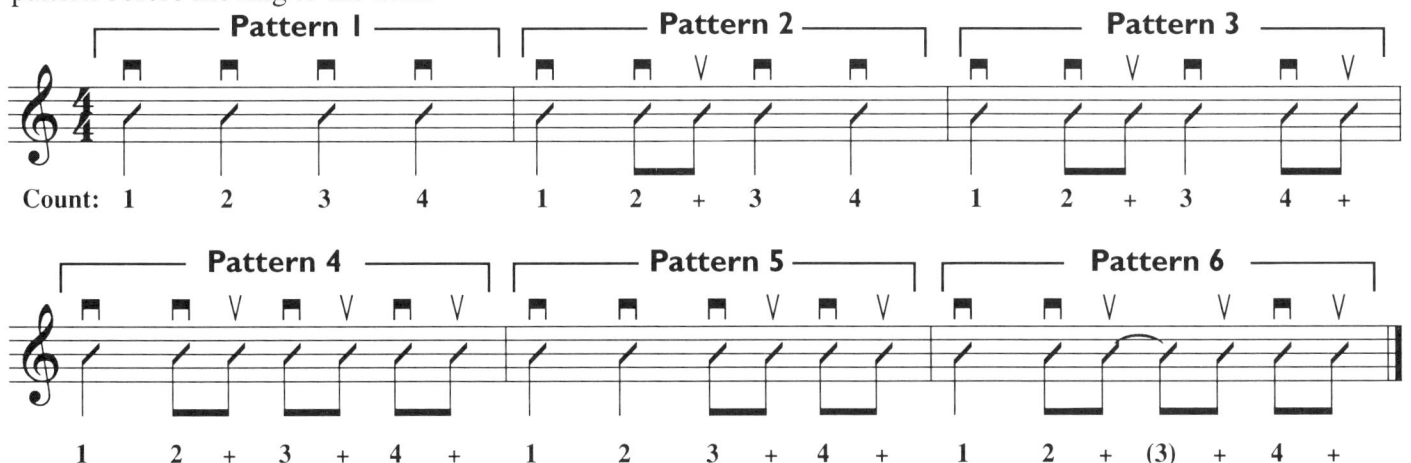

13

Notice pattern 6 contains a loop called a "tie." When two strum bars are connected with a tie, play the first strum and allow it to ring through the time value of the second. Do not strum the second strum bar.

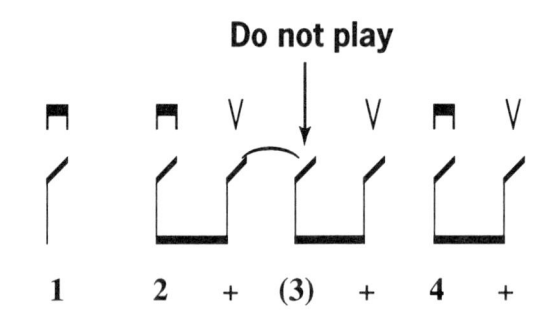

This :| is a repeat sign. When it appears, go to the double bar with the dots on the right |: and play that portion of the piece again. If there is not a set of double bars with dots on the right, repeat the beginning of the piece.

Practice the following three blues progressions. In each measure, use the strum pattern which is written is the first measure of the example.

Simile means to continue playing each measure in a similar manner as the preceding measure.

Practice the following song using strum patterns for 4/4. Once a pattern has been selected, play the same pattern in each measure. Repeat the song several times using a different pattern for 4/4 each time.

Baby Don't Love Me

| E7 | A7 | E7 | |

I love my ba - by, ___ but my ba - by don't love me.

| A7 | | E7 | |

I love my ba - by, ___ but my ba - by don't love me.

| B7 | A7 | E7 | |

Feel - in' down and lone - ly. ___ Wish these blues would set me free.

Ain't Got a Nickel

| E7 | A7 | E7 | |

Ain't got a nick - el. ___ Ain't got a pen - ny to my name.

| A7 | | E7 | |

Ain't got a nick - el. ___ Ain't got a pen - ny to my name.

| B7 | A7 | E7 | |

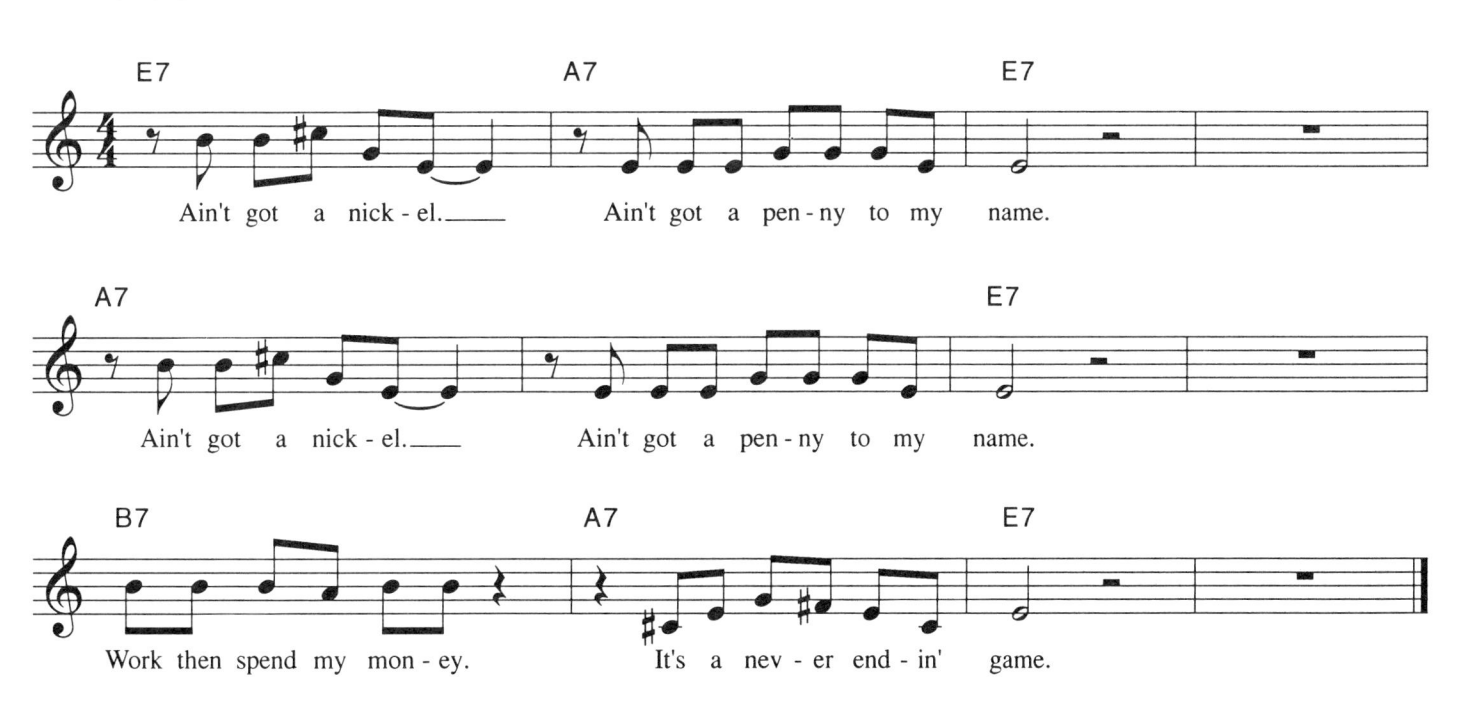

Work then spend my mon - ey. It's a nev - er end - in' game.

Building the Blues

The chords most commonly used in the blues are the I, IV, and V chords. The Roman numeral I is used to represent the key of the song. For example, the I chord in the key of A is A. The IV chord is four steps up the major scale (usually four names up the alphabet) from the I chord. For example, the IV chord in the key of A is D. The V chord is five steps up the major scale (alphabet) from the I chord. The V chord in the key of A is E. Seventh (7) chords are commonly used for every chord in the blues. Seventh chords are used because they have a dissonant, off-key sound to them. This dissonance reflects how one might feel when having the blues.

The chart below lists the I, IV, and V chords in some of the basic keys. The fingerings for these chords are found at the back of this book. By learning the blues progression using Roman numerals, the correct chords may be inserted and the blues can be played in any key.

	I	IV	V
Easiest keys for open chords	C7	F7	G7
	G7	C7	D7
	D7	G7	A7
	A7	D7	E7
	E7	A7	B7
Keys using moveable power chords	B7	E7	F#7
	F#7	B7	C#7
	D♭7	G♭7	A♭7
	A♭7	D♭7	E♭7
	E♭7	A♭7	B♭7
	B♭7	E♭7	F7
	F7	B♭7	C7

The formula for constructing the standard 12-bar blues progression is: four measures of the I chord, two measures of the IV chord, two measures of the I chord, one measure of the V chord, one measure of the IV chord, and two measures of the I chord. This basic progression is written below. The chords in parentheses show what chords would be in the key of A. Practice playing this progression using any one of the strum patterns for 4/4.

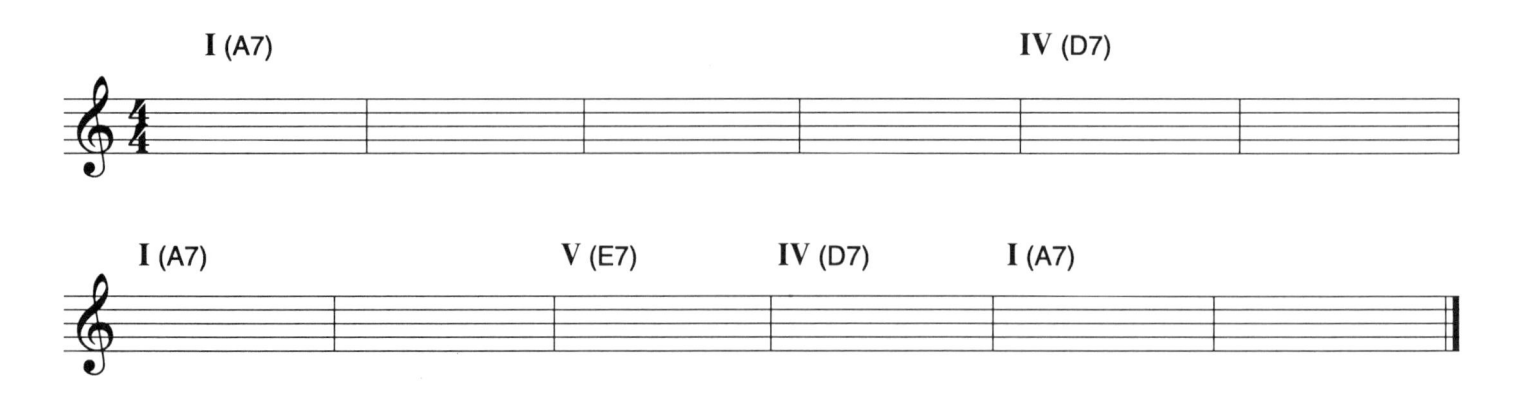

I (A7)   IV (D7)

I (A7)   V (E7)   IV (D7)   I (A7)

fretboard diagram – first 12 frets

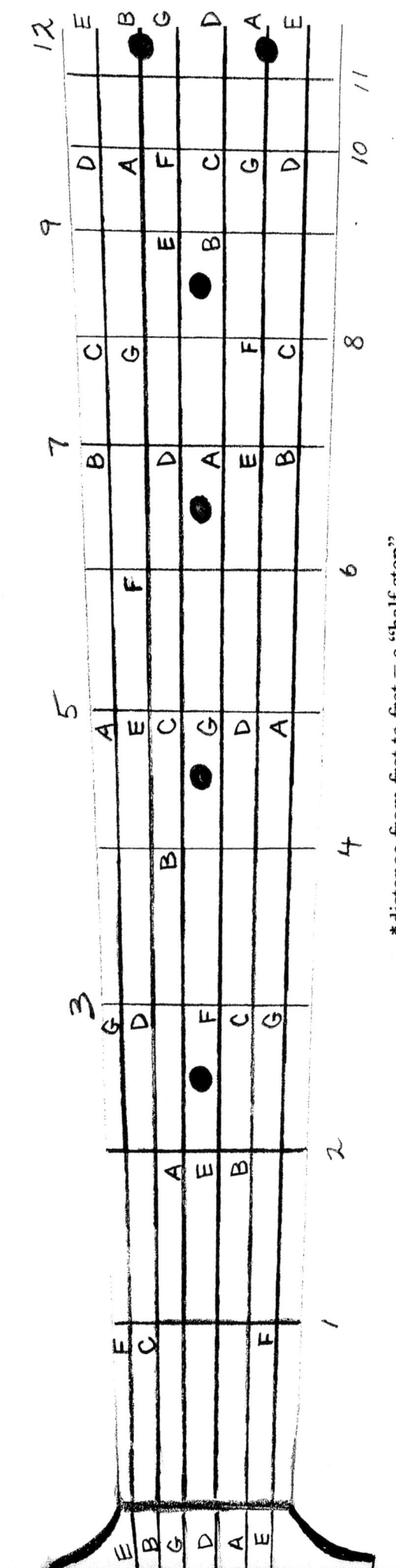

*distance from fret to fret = a "half step"
*distance 2 frets apart = a "whole step"

*the only *natural* half steps are between **E / F** and **B / C**

*a "flat" note is exactly one half step below (one fret to the left of) its natural value
*a "sharp" note is exactly one half step above (one fret to the right of) its natural value
*the note between any two notes that are a whole step apart (such as **F** and **G**) can be called either "sharp" or "flat" (in this case **F - sharp** or **G - flat**), depending on what diatonic key you are playing in… (in other words **F#** and **Gb** share the exact same fret and sound exactly the same, but technically they belong to different musical keys)

There are many variations of the 12-bar blues progression. One of the most common is written below. Notice the IV chord has been added in the second measure and the V chord is added in the last measure. The V chord in the last measure signals the repeat of the progression and is called the **turnaround**. After repeating the progression, end by strumming the I chord one time. Practice this and the previous blues progression in several keys. It is essential these progressions be memorized. Use any one of the strum patterns for 4/4.

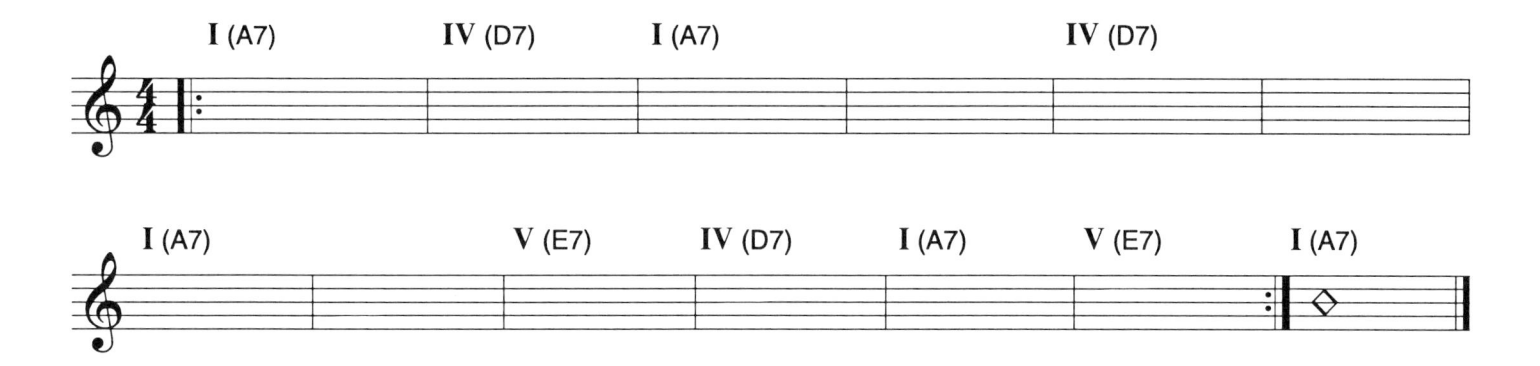

I (A7)   IV (D7)   I (A7)   IV (D7)

I (A7)   V (E7)   IV (D7)   I (A7)   V (E7)   I (A7)

Practice the following song in several keys by inserting the correct I, IV, and V chords for the selected key. Notice the lyrics are given, but the melody is not written. Use the lyrics and make up a melody to fit the key.

Set Me Free

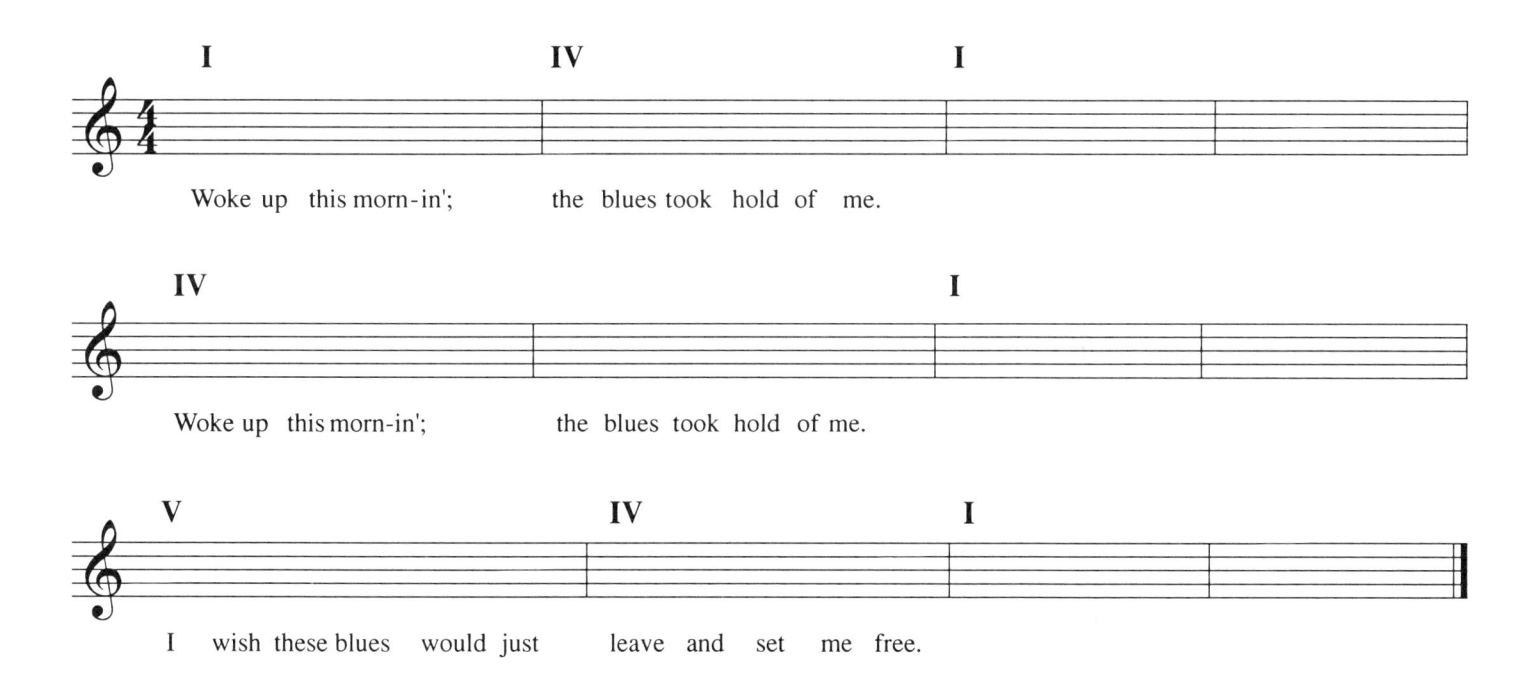

I   IV   I

Woke up this morn-in';   the blues took hold of me.

IV   I

Woke up this morn-in';   the blues took hold of me.

V   IV   I

I wish these blues would just   leave and set me free.

Minor Blues

When playing the blues in a minor key, the Roman numeral formula can still be used, but the i and iv chords become minor and are represented by small Roman numerals. The V chord remains a seventh chord. Written below is a minor blues in the key of A minor. Practice strumming this progression using one of the strum patterns for 4/4. Fingerings for the minor chords can be found on page 40.

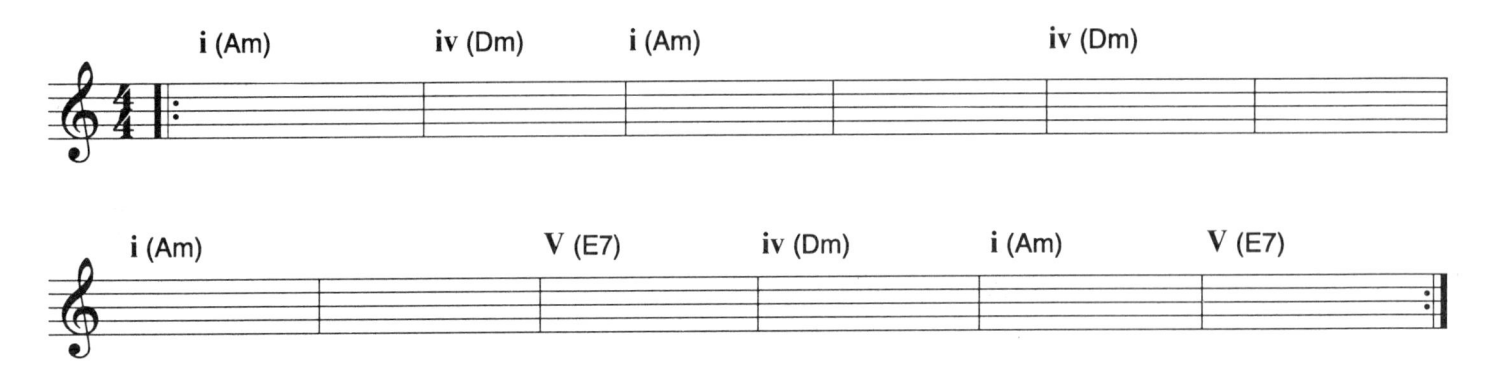

Practice the following song which is a blues in the key of A minor.

Sun Won't Shine

Sun won't shine, since my ba-by went a-way.

Sun won't shine, since my ba-by went a-way.

Clouds won't leave, 'til my ba-by's back to stay.

How to Read Standard Notation

Being able to read and write music in standard notation will be a great asset to any guitarist. Understanding standard notation makes it easier for guitarists to learn new music (especially if a recording is not available), write their ideas for other guitarists to play, and jot down ideas they may want to remember in the future.

The lines and spaces on which notes are written is called the **staff**. Guitar music is written in the **treble clef**. The treble clef sign will be at the beginning of the staff. The treble clef circles and identifies the second line from the botton as G. The treble clef is sometimes called the **G clef**.

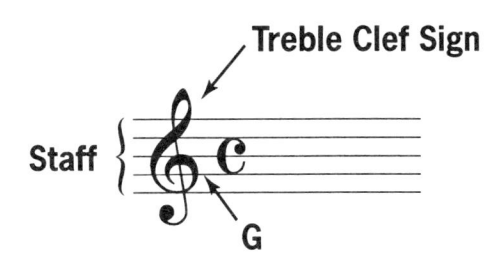

The note names for the treble clef are shown on the staff below. The mnemonic (memory building) device commonly used to remember the notes on the lines of the treble clef is *Every Good Boy Does Fine*. The letters found in the spaces of the treble clef spell the word *FACE*.

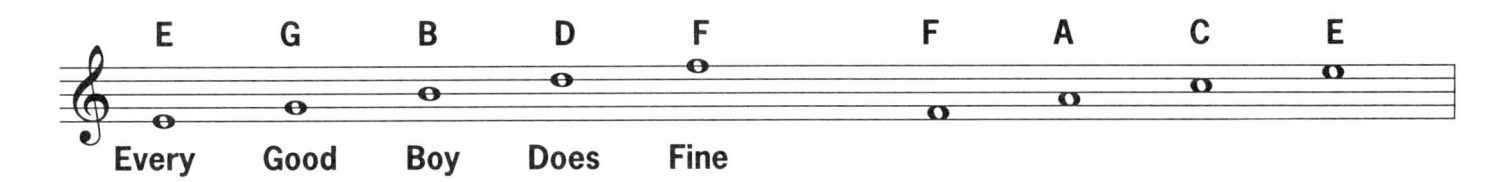

The time values are the same for standard notation as they are for strumming notation. Time values for each note and rest are shown below for common time (C) signatures with a four as the bottom number (4/4, 3/4, 2/4 etc.)

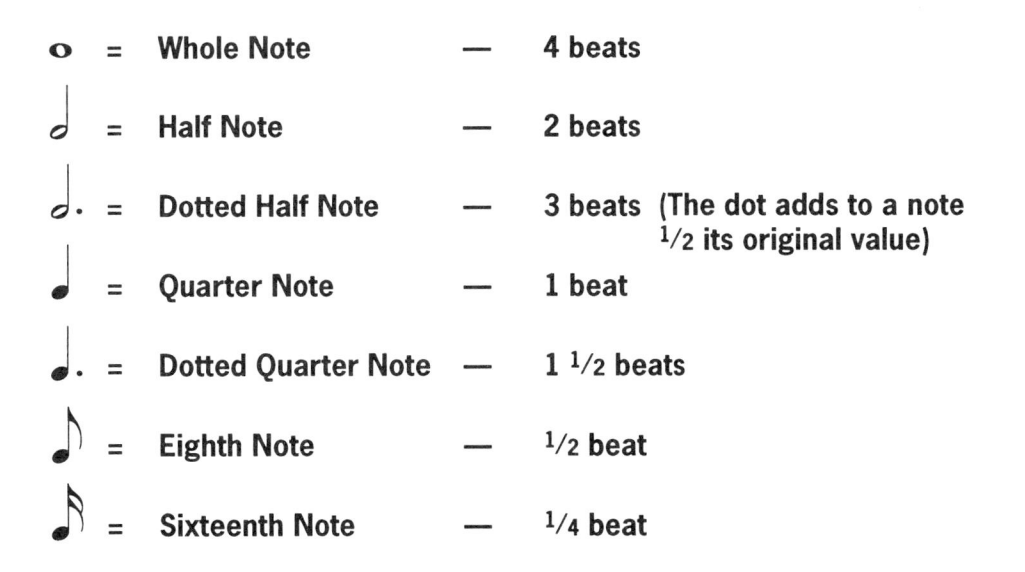

o	=	Whole Note	—	4 beats
𝅗𝅥	=	Half Note	—	2 beats
𝅗𝅥.	=	Dotted Half Note	—	3 beats (The dot adds to a note 1/2 its original value)
♩	=	Quarter Note	—	1 beat
♩.	=	Dotted Quarter Note	—	1 1/2 beats
♪	=	Eighth Note	—	1/2 beat
𝅘𝅥𝅯	=	Sixteenth Note	—	1/4 beat

| Whole Rest 4 beats | Half Rest 2 beats | Dotted Half Rest 3 beats | Quarter Rest 1 beat | Dotted Quarter Rest 1 1/2 beats | Eighth Rest 1/2 beat | Sixteenth Rest 1/4 beat |

Standard Notation in First Position

While there are many notes on the guitar (one note for each string and fret), only standard notation in first position will be covered in this book. The term **first position** means that the first finger of the left hand will be stationed or positioned at the first fret and will, therefore, play all the notes on each string located in that fret. This allows each of the left-hand fingers to play in the fret that corresponds with the finger number. The second finger is responsible for all of the notes in the second fret; the third finger plays the notes in the third fret and the fourth finger will play the notes found in the fourth fret. When playing in a higher position, the first finger determines the position, and the other fingers correspond to the frets just as they did in first position. For example, to play in the fifth position, the first finger of the left hand is stationed at the fifth fret, the second finger in the sixth fret, the third finger in the seventh fret and the fourth finger in the eighth fret. Sometimes a Roman numeral is used in music and chord diagrams to indicate a position or fret number.

Notes on the First String

The notes on the first string are shown below. They are E, F, and G. This following exercise will help in the memorization of these notes.

Position – I

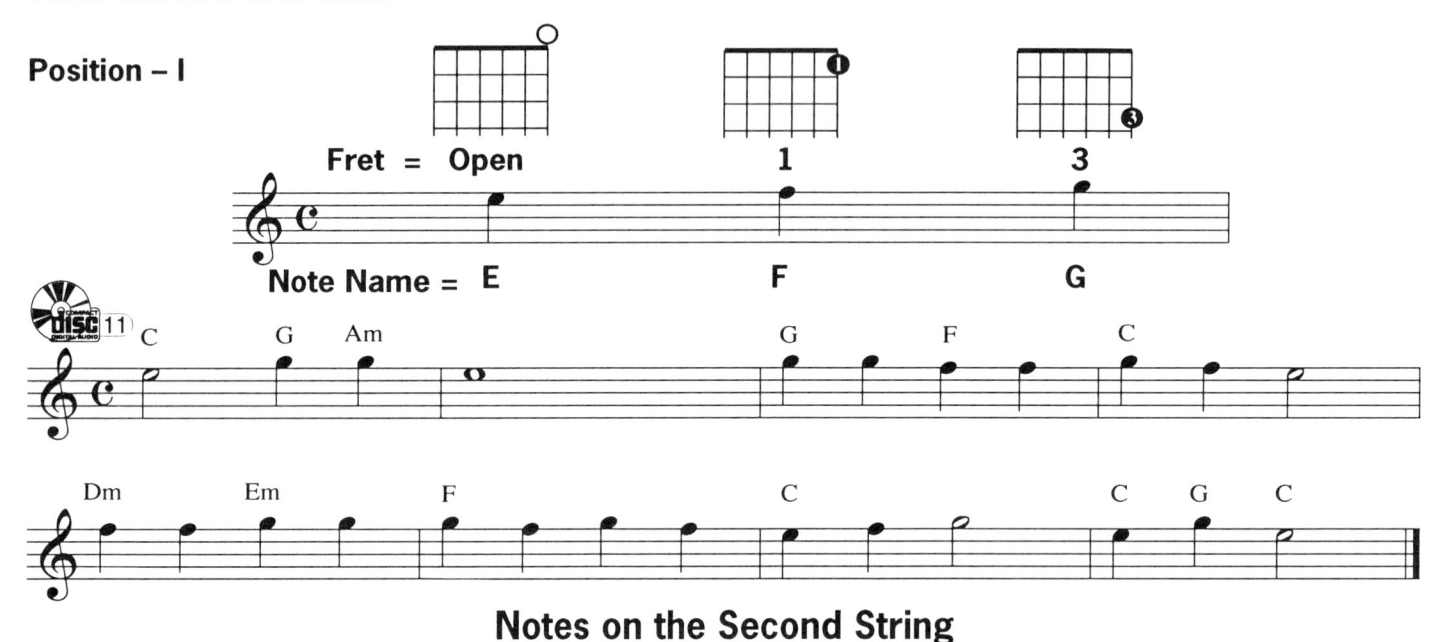

Fret = Open, 1, 3
Note Name = E, F, G

Notes on the Second String

The notes on the second string are shown below. They are B, C, and D. This following exercise will help in the memorization of these notes.

Position – I

Fret = Open, 1, 3
Note Name = B, C, D

20

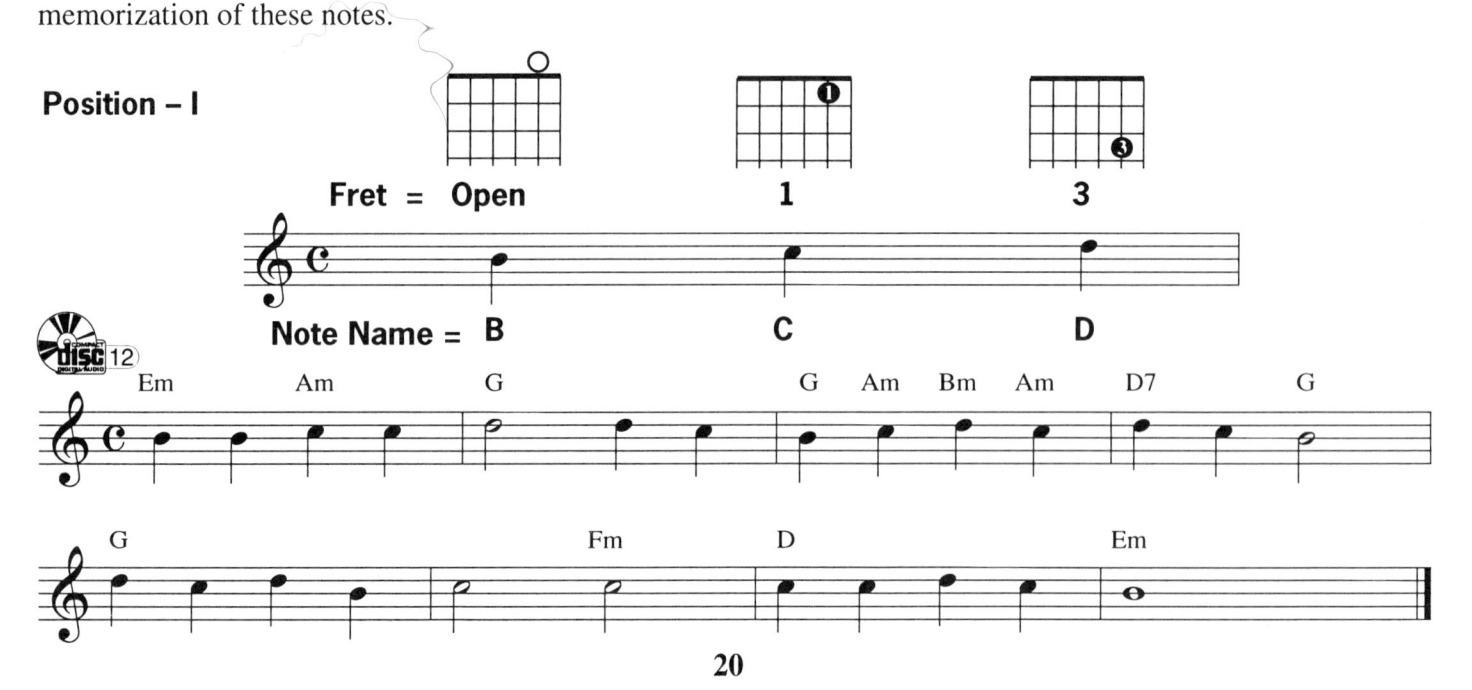

Play the following blues solos to learn the notes on the first two strings. The chords above the staff are the accompaniment guitar part.

Mama's Cookin'

Accompaniment guitar part

No Time to Practice Blues

When playing eighth notes, alternate picking (down-up picking) is used (♫♫). "I Got No Money" makes use of eighth notes and ties.

I Got No Money

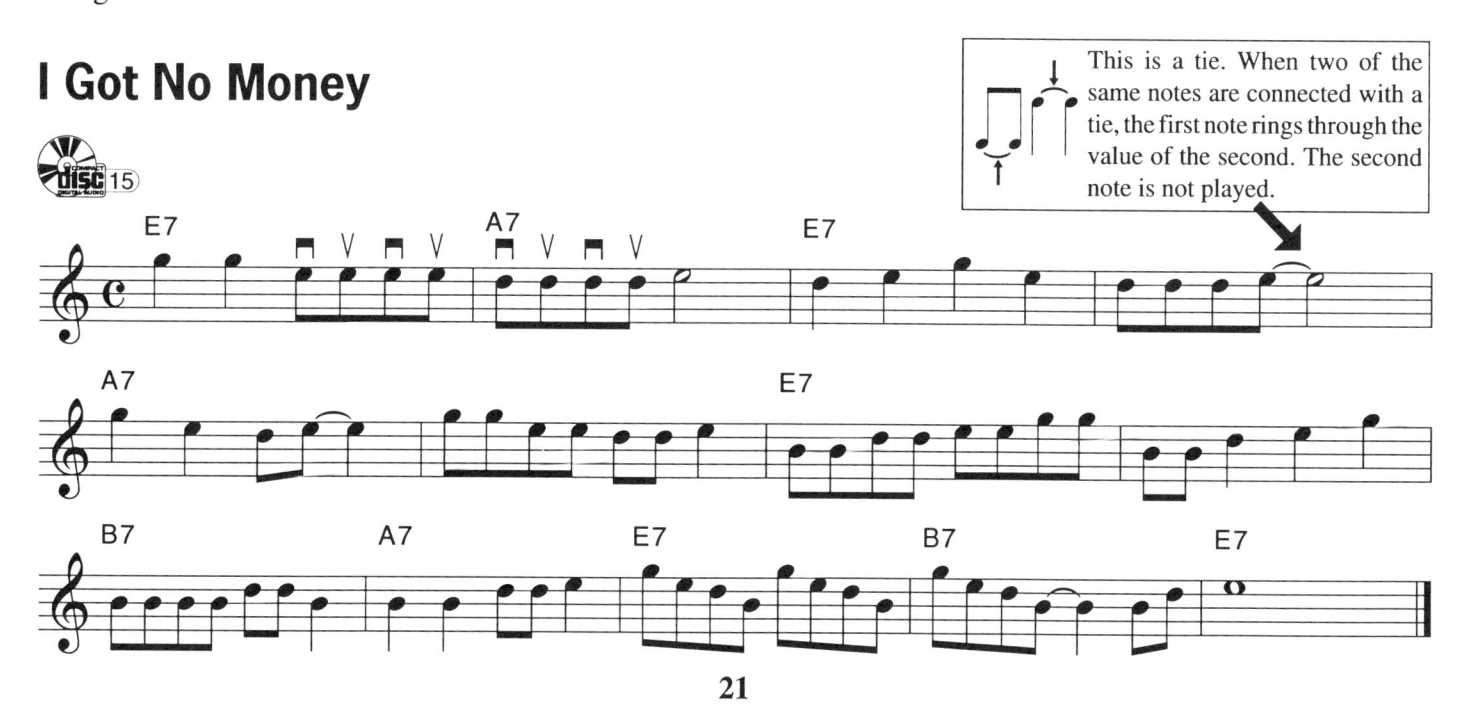

This is a tie. When two of the same notes are connected with a tie, the first note rings through the value of the second. The second note is not played.

Notes on the Third String

The notes G and A are found on the third string.

Position – I

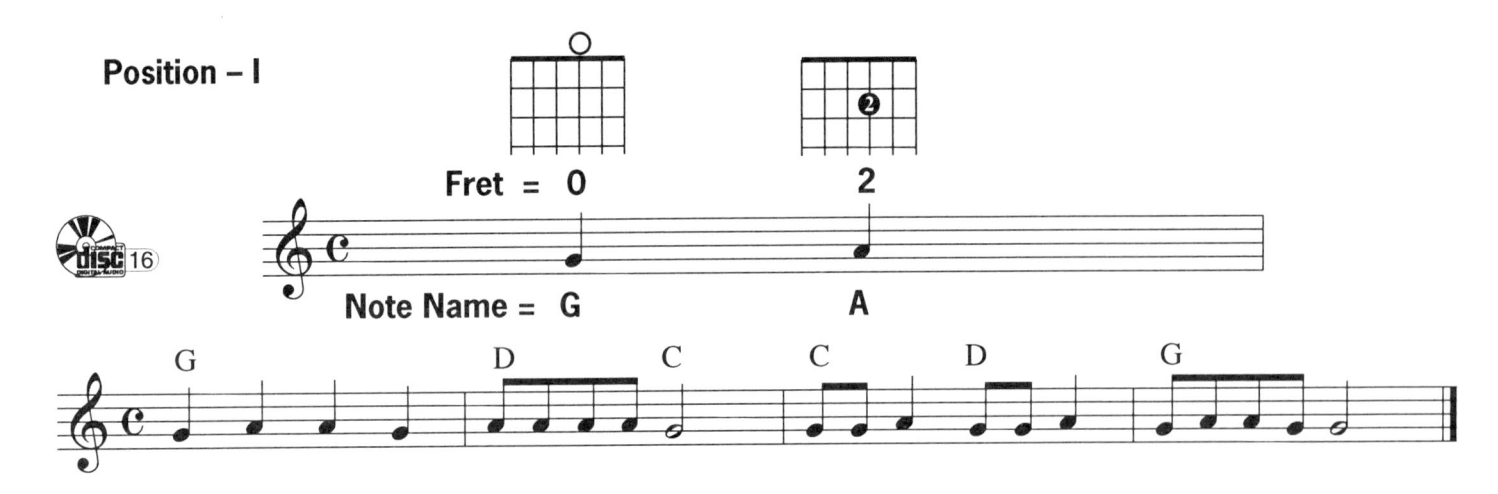

Fret = 0   2

Note Name = G   A

Play the following blues melody that uses the notes found on the first three strings.

Help Yourself

Notes on the Fourth String

The notes on the fourth string are D, E, and F.

Position – I

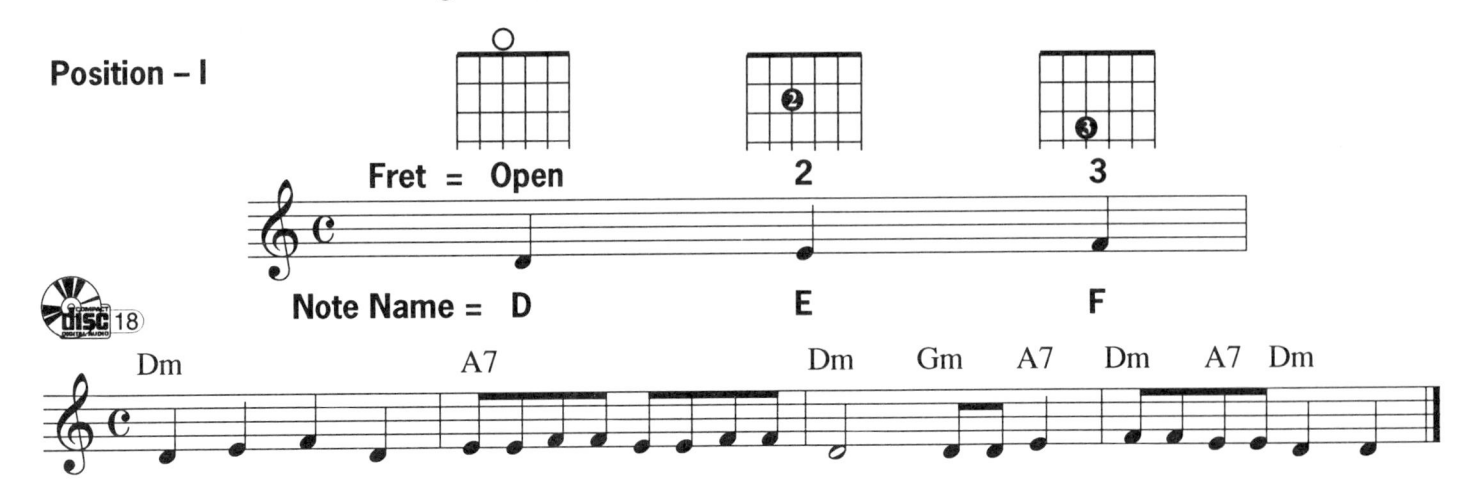

Fret = Open   2   3

Note Name = D   E   F

Play this blues melody which uses the notes found on strings two, three, and four.

Seven Minus Three

Acc. guitar part

Accidentals

An accidental is a sign that alters the pitch of a note. The sharp sign (♯), flat sign (♭) and natural sign (♮) are all accidentals. When a sharp sign appears in front of a note, the note is raised one fret (one half step). If an F on the first string has a sharp sign in front of it, move one fret higher (toward the body of the guitar). The note, F-sharp, will be played on the first string, second fret. If an open note (a note that is usually played on an open string) is sharped, play the note in the first fret of the same string. When playing notes with accidentals, be sure the finger number matches the fret number.

When a note has an accidental, the accidental affects **all** of the same notes in the remainder of that measure only. After that measure, the accidental is negated and the notes return to their original pitch. A natural sign in front of a note cancels the sharp or flat.

Fret: 0 4 0 4 0 4 3 2 0 4 4 0

Practice the following blues solo which contains sharps.

Dark Side of a Dream

When a flat sign appears in front of a note (♭♩), the note is lowered one fret (one half step). For example, if a D on the second string has a flat sign in front of it, play it one fret lower (toward the head of the guitar). The note D-flat will be played on the second string, second fret. If an open note has a flat in front of it, the note must be moved to a lower string as an open string cannot be lowered without retuning. To flat an open note, place a finger on the next lower string in the fret that matches the pitch of the note on the open string. Then flat the note by lowering it one fret. A chart showing the location of all the flatted open notes is shown below.

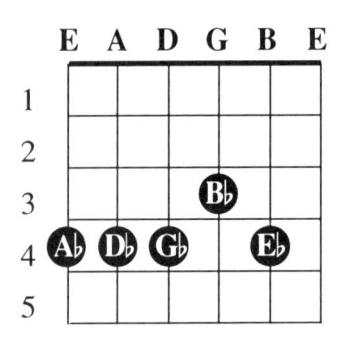

Practice the following blues solo which contains flats.

Freezing Point

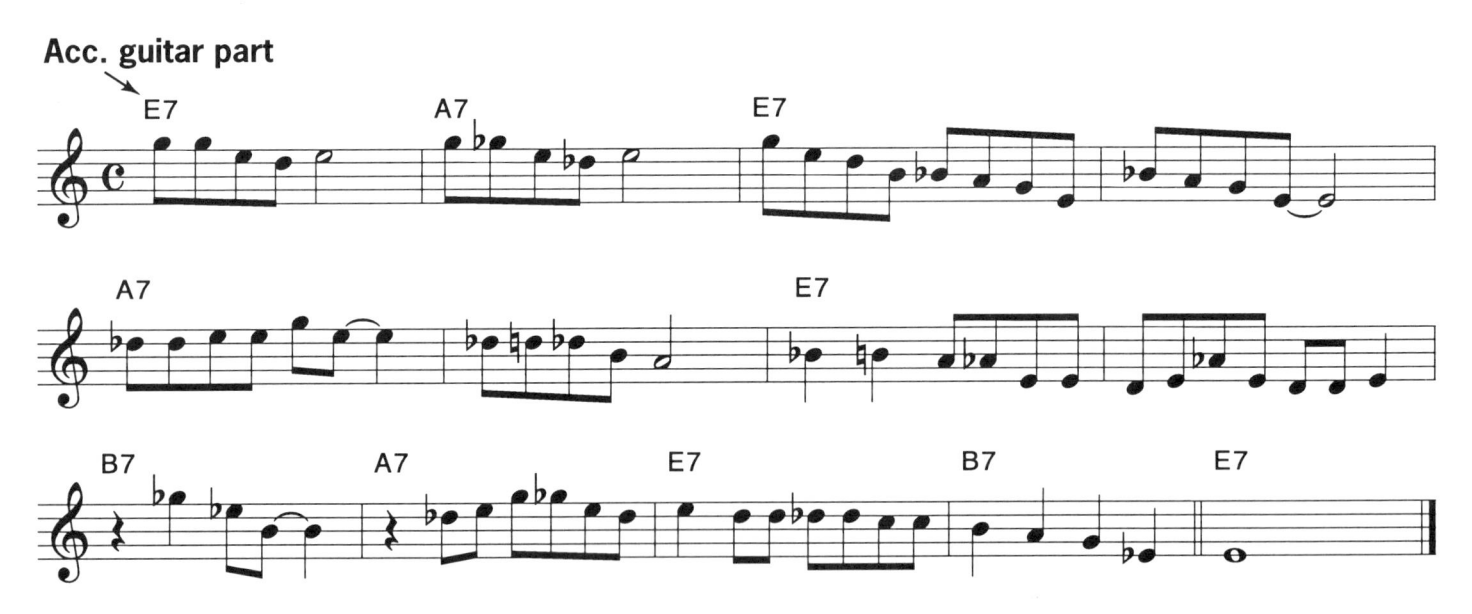

Notes on the Fifth String

The notes on the fifth string are written below. Remember, use the same left-hand finger number as the fret number.

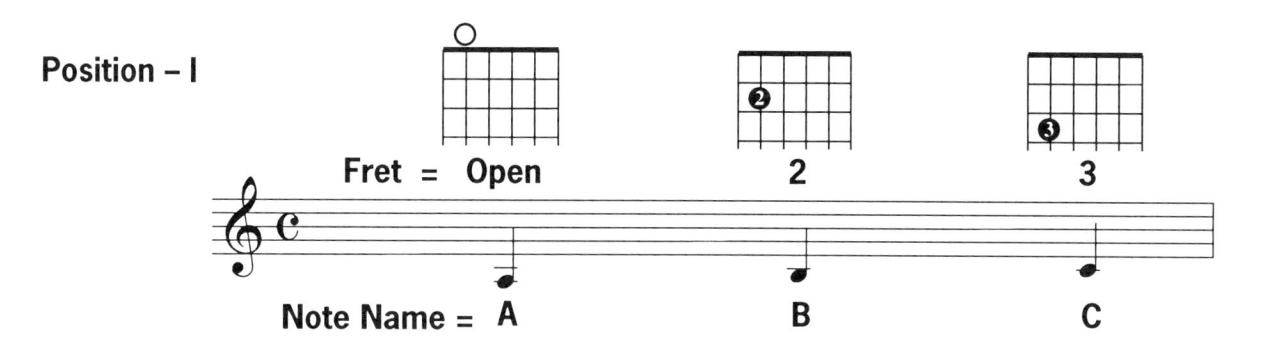

Position – I

Fret = Open, 2, 3

Note Name = A, B, C

Practice the following exercise which uses only the notes on the fifth string.

Practice the following blues solo which uses only the notes on the fifth string.

Double Trouble

Notes on the Sixth String

Written below are the notes on the sixth string.

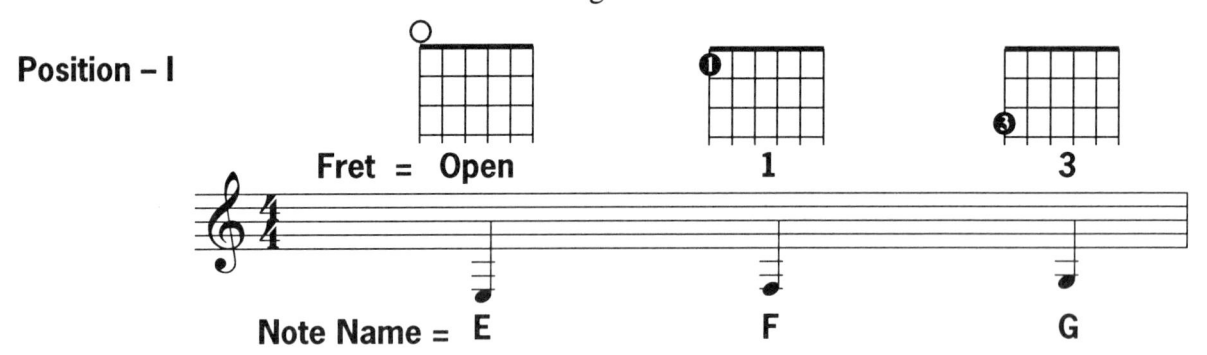

Position – I

Fret = Open   1   3

Note Name = E   F   G

Practice the following exercise using only the notes on the sixth string.

Practice the following blues solo which uses only the notes on the sixth string.

Long Road Home

Eighth Rest. Rest for 1/2 beat. The note following this rest sign is played on the second half of the beat and is played with an up-stroke.

The following blues solo uses a combination of notes on the fifth and sixth strings.

Cry, Baby

The next blues solo uses notes on strings five and six combined with notes on other strings. This blues solo is a good example of how a blues guitarist might play a bass line (bass part).

Things Ain't the Same

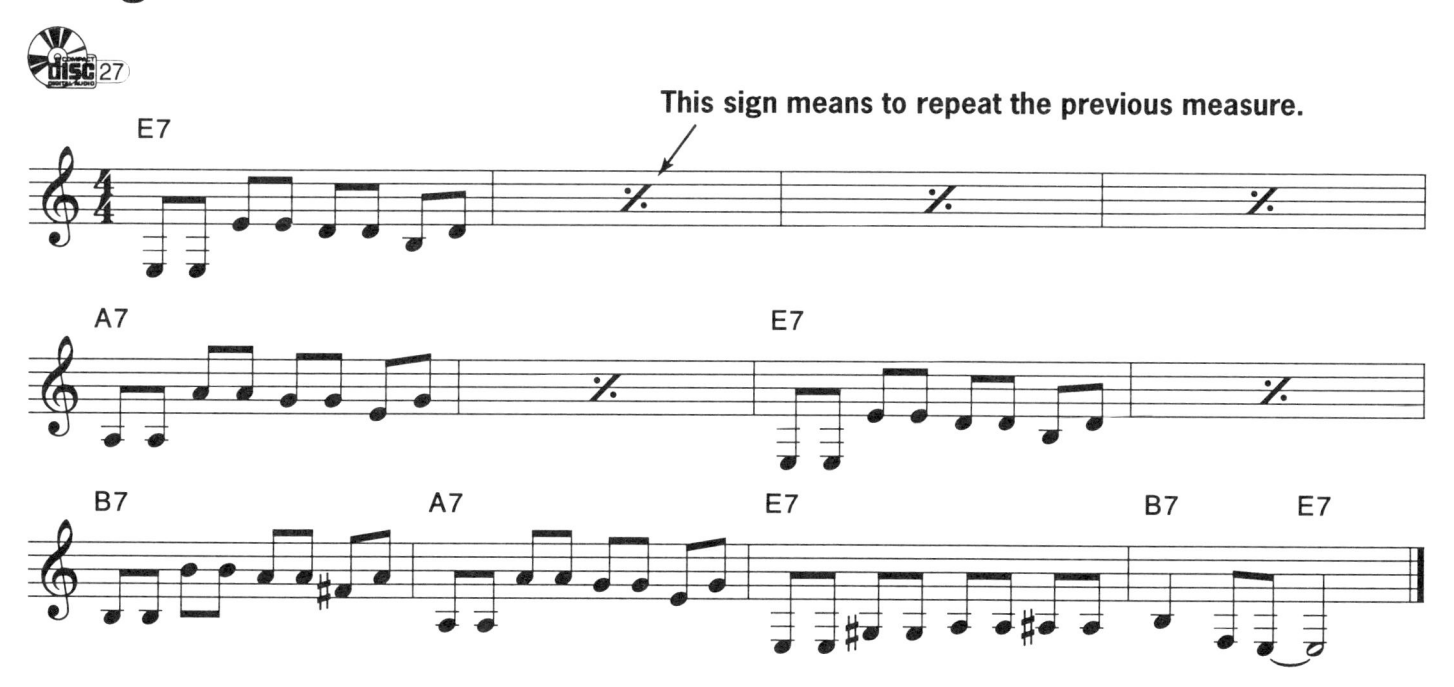

This sign means to repeat the previous measure.

27

Power Chords

Power chords are **two-note chords** that are written with a 5 next to the chord name (A5). When playing power chords, be sure to pick both notes quickly so they sound simultaneously. Chord diagrams for the A, D, and E open power chords are shown below. In the blues, power chords are often used in place of seventh chords.

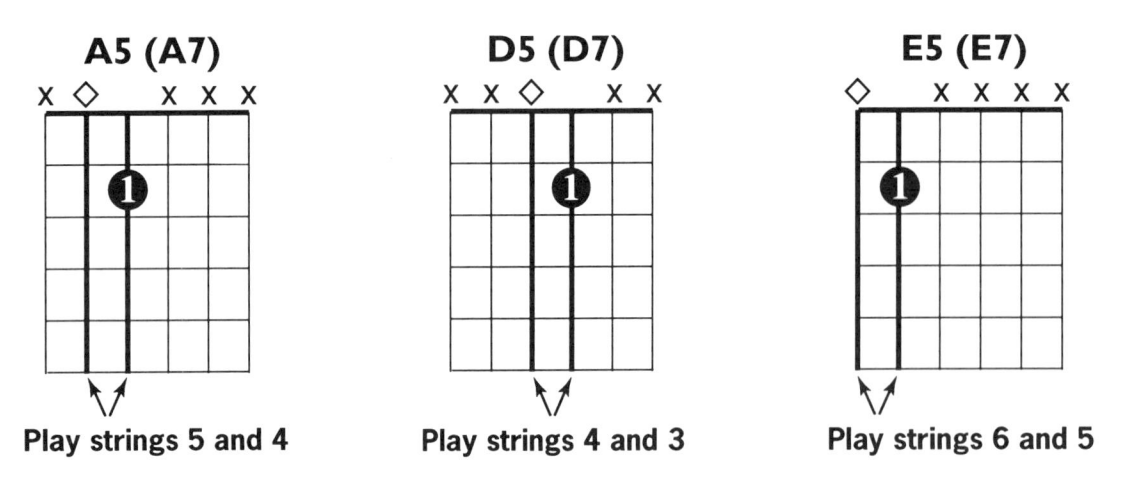

A5 (A7) — Play strings 5 and 4

D5 (D7) — Play strings 4 and 3

E5 (E7) — Play strings 6 and 5

Play the following blues which uses open power chords. Even though eighth notes are used for this power chord strum pattern, use down-strokes only.

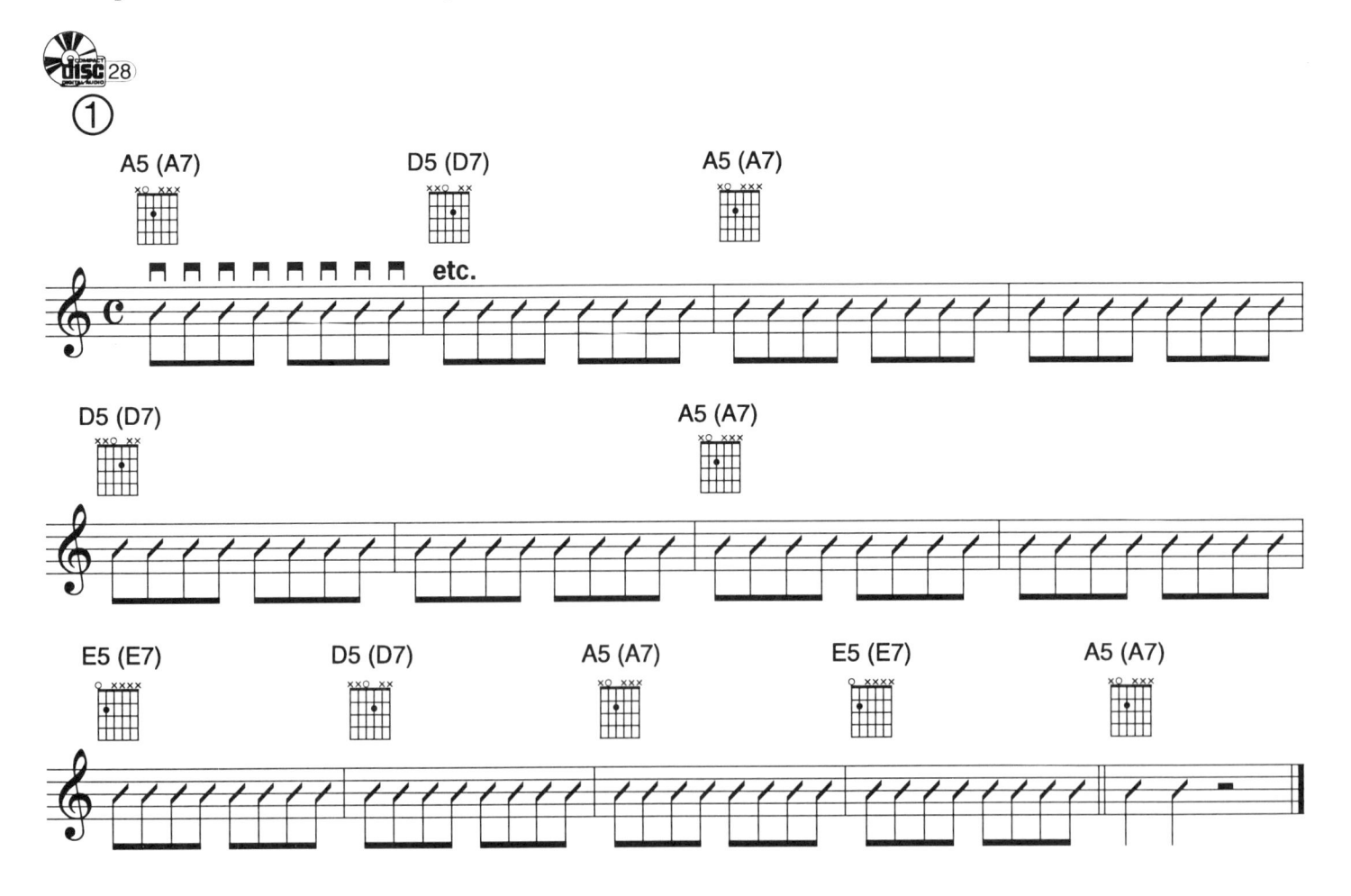

①

A5 (A7)	D5 (D7)	A5 (A7)	A5 (A7)
D5 (D7)	D5 (D7)	A5 (A7)	A5 (A7)
E5 (E7)	D5 (D7)	A5 (A7)	E5 (E7)	A5 (A7)

Add the Sixth

A common variation on the power chord involves adding a finger on the third and seventh down-strokes (on the second and fourth beats) of the measure. For example, on the A5 chord, play strings 5 and 4 together four times. Use only down-strokes. On the third stroke, add the left-hand third finger where the "3" is drawn on the diagram below. On the fourth stroke, lift the third finger. Do this twice in each measure.

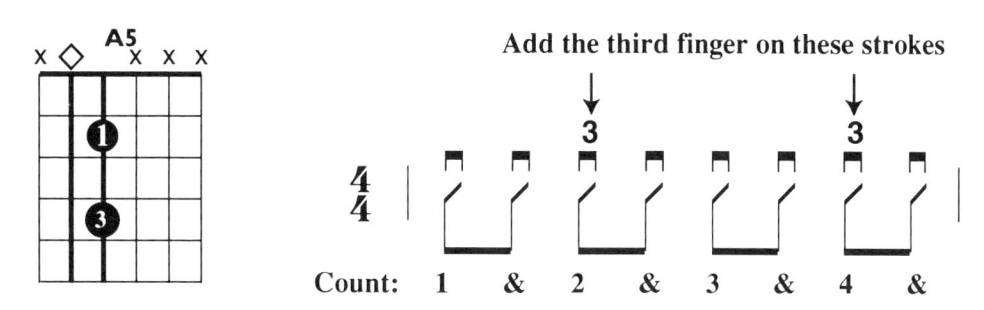

This technique could be used on the D5 chord by adding the third finger on the third string where the "X3" is drawn.

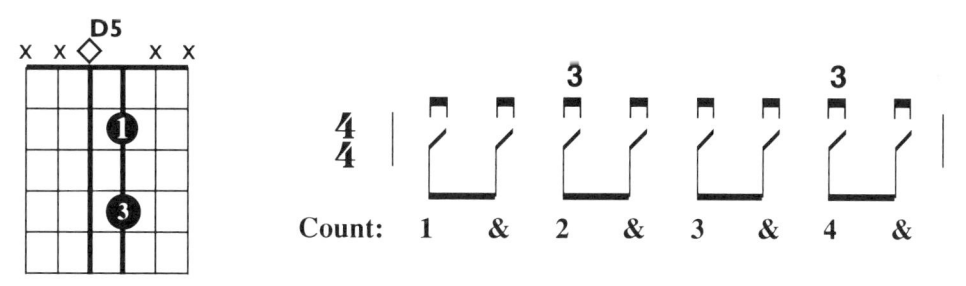

For the E5, add the third finger in the fourth fret on the fifth string.

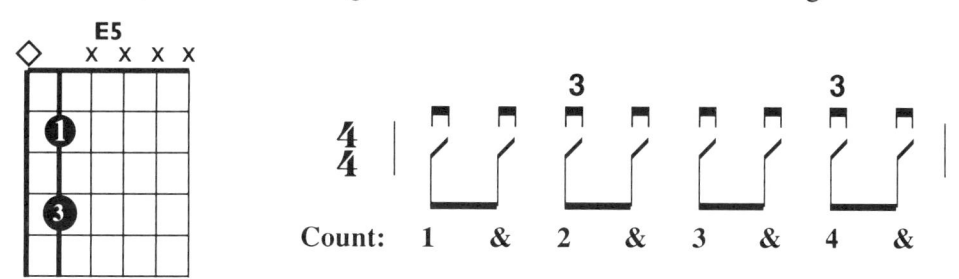

Play this twelve-bar blues which uses the variations on the power chord.

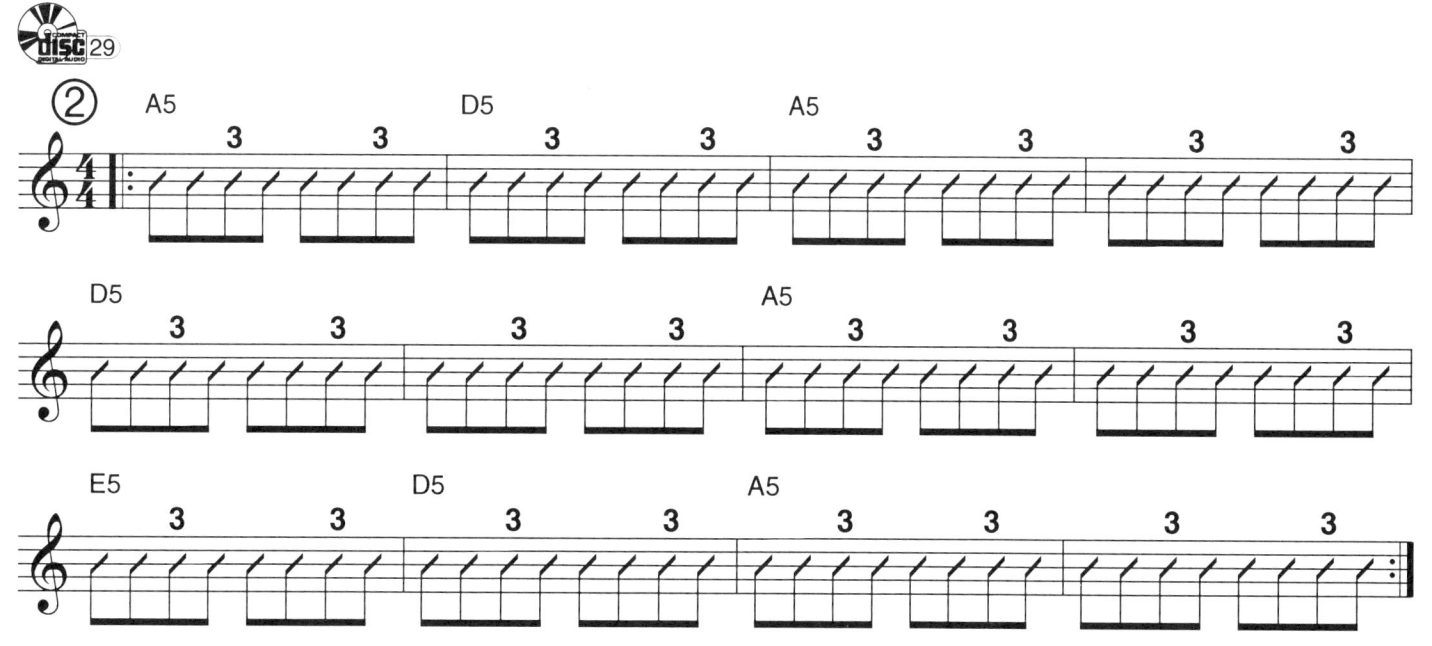

29

Moveable power chords allow guitarists to easily play the blues in any key. The diagrams below show power chords with the root on the sixth and fifth string. The root is the note that names the chord. An A is the root in any type of A chord (A7, Am, etc.). A chart has also been provided for easy location of every note on the sixth and fifth strings. Remember, to sharp a note raise the note one fret. To flat a note, lower the note one fret.

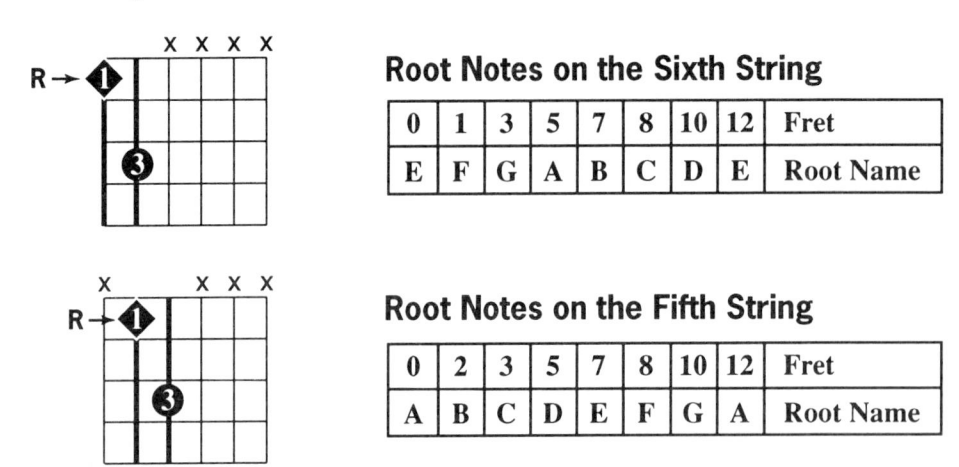

Root Notes on the Sixth String

0	1	3	5	7	8	10	12	Fret
E	F	G	A	B	C	D	E	Root Name

Root Notes on the Fifth String

0	2	3	5	7	8	10	12	Fret
A	B	C	D	E	F	G	A	Root Name

Practice the following blues using moveable power chords. The R5 and R6 indicate whether the chord is to be played on the fifth string or the sixth string.

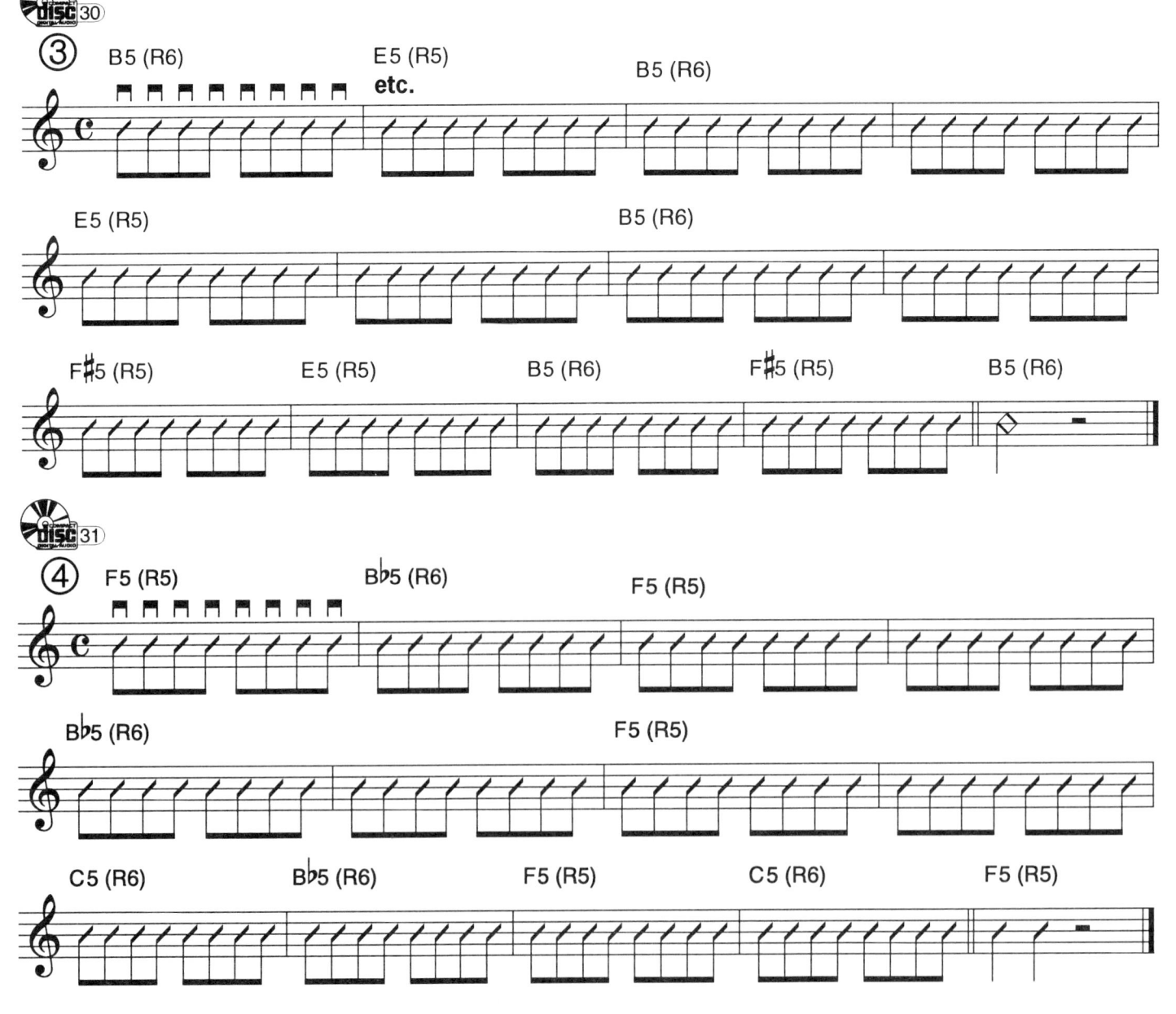

Track 30

③ B5 (R6) | E5 (R5) etc. | B5 (R6) | B5 (R6)

E5 (R5) | E5 (R5) | B5 (R6) | B5 (R6)

F#5 (R5) | E5 (R5) | B5 (R6) | F#5 (R5) | B5 (R6)

Track 31

④ F5 (R5) | Bb5 (R6) | F5 (R5) | F5 (R5)

Bb5 (R6) | Bb5 (R6) | F5 (R5) | F5 (R5)

C5 (R6) | Bb5 (R6) | F5 (R5) | C5 (R6) | F5 (R5)

30

Tablature

Another way of writing guitar music is called tablature. The six horizontal lines represent the strings on a guitar. The top line is the first string.

1st String

Strings

A number on a line indicates in which fret to place a left-hand finger. A stem connected to the number shows the note gets one beat.

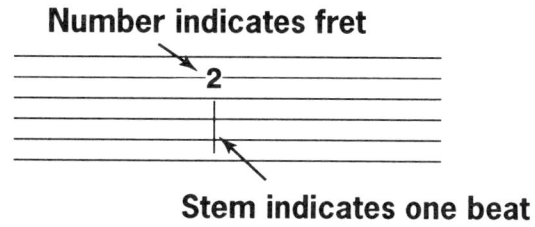

Number indicates fret

Stem indicates one beat

In the example below, the finger would be placed on the first string in the third fret.

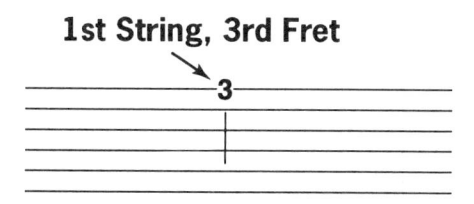

1st String, 3rd Fret

If two or more numbers are written on top of one another, play the strings at the same time.

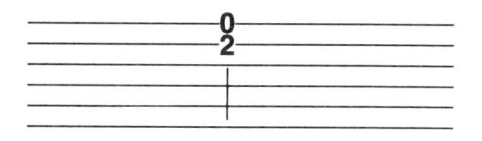

Note Values in Tablature

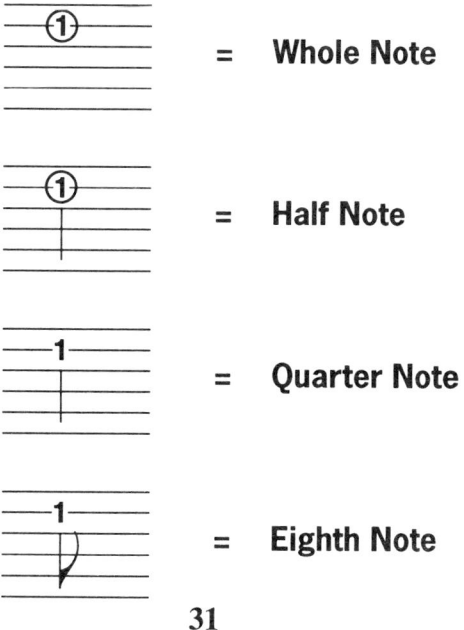

= Whole Note

= Half Note

= Quarter Note

= Eighth Note

31

Because the notes used in the solos for this section of the book are taken from scale patterns, and some patterns explore upper positions on the fretboard, the musical examples for this section of this book will be presented in tablature.

Minor Pentatonic and Blues Scales

Below are diagrams for the E and A minor pentatonic scales in first (open) position.

E Minor Pentatonic ← **Open Strings** → **A Minor Pentatonic**

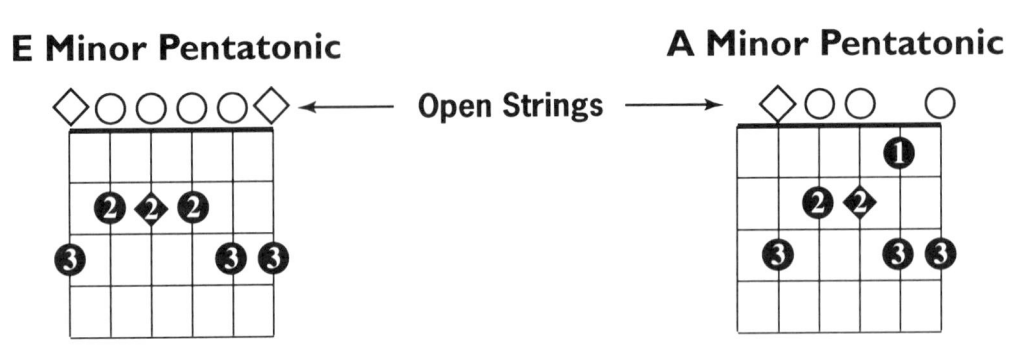

Many guitarists use the minor pentatonic scale to create melodies and improvised solos over blues progressions. Use the E minor pentatonic scale when playing a blues in the key of E. Use the A minor pentatonic scale when playing solos in the key of A. The minor pentatonic scale used for the solo should have the same letter name as the key. This "key scale" is used to solo over the entire progression (even when the chords change). The solos below make use of the E and A minor pentatonic scale and demonstrate how a guitarist can use these scales to write melodies or play an improvised solo.

Solo 1

Strum as a chord

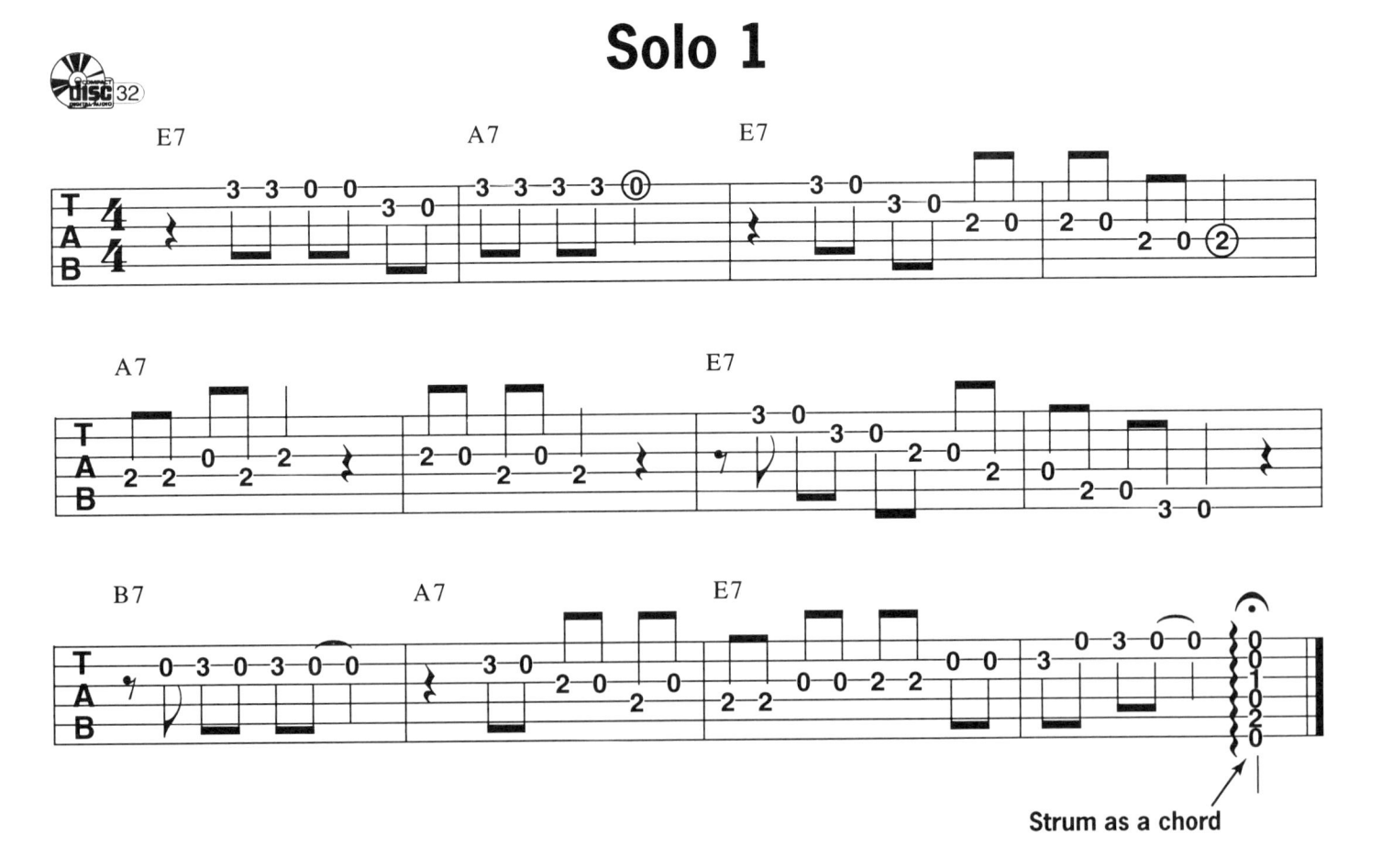

Solo 2

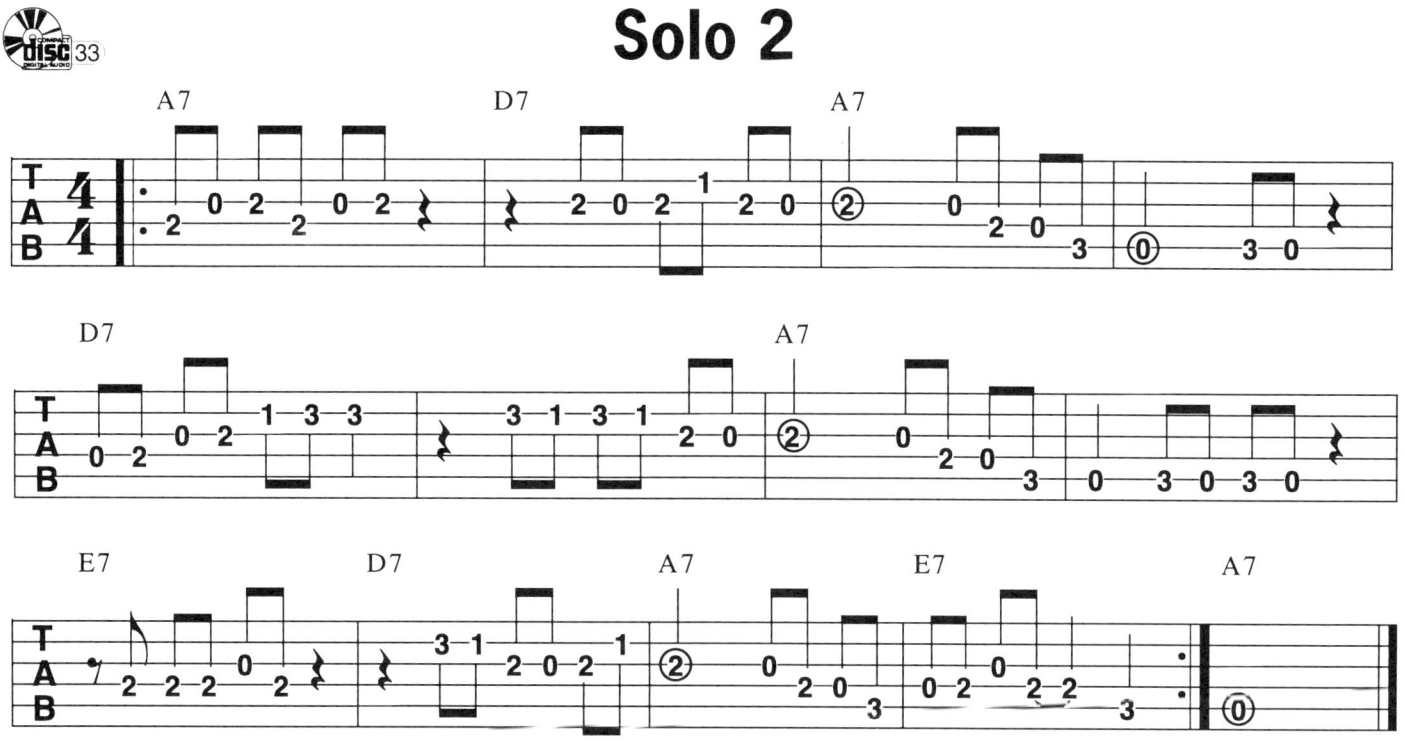

The blues scale has one more note per octave than the minor pentatonic scale. Some refer to this note as the **blue note** because it can have a harsh, dissonant sound. Diagrams for the open E and A blues scale are shown below. The circled numbers show the locations of the blue notes.

E Blues Scale

A Blues Scale

The blues scale can be used just as the minor pentatonic scale can be used to write blues melodies and play improvised blues solos. The solos below demonstrate how the blues scale can be used. As with the minor pentatonic scale, use the E blues scale for blues in the key of E and the A blues scale for blues in the key of A.

Blues E

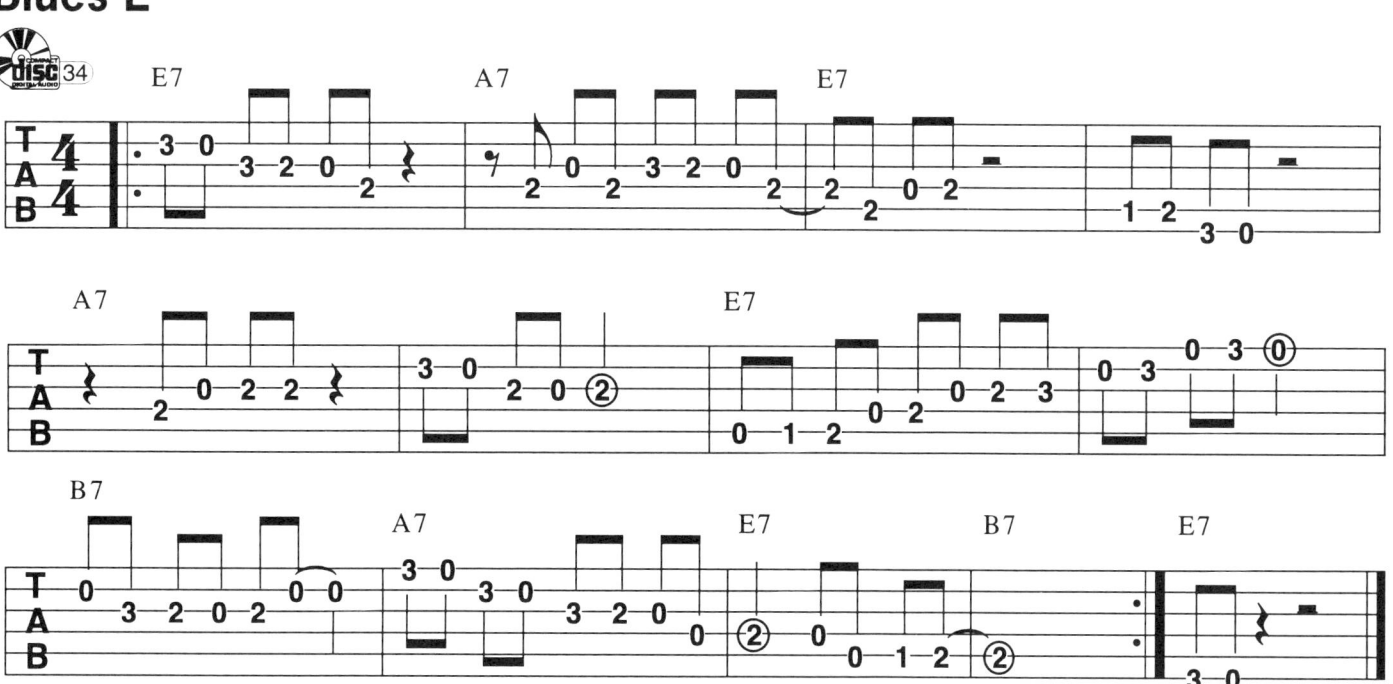

Blues A

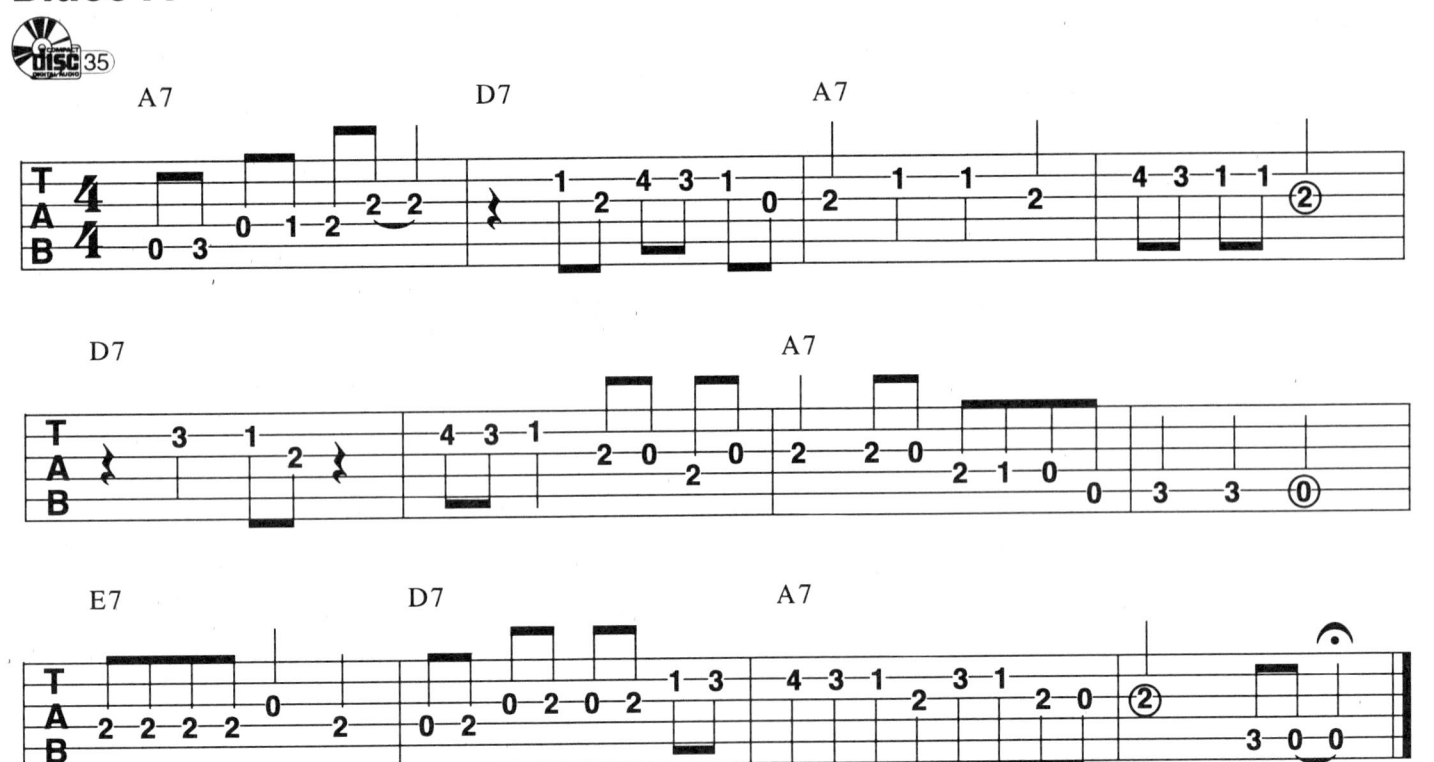

Moveable Minor Pentatonic Scale

Drawn below is a minor pentatonic scale which can be moved up and down the neck. The pattern can begin in any fret. This scale pattern has the "root" on the sixth string. The **root** is the note which names the scale. The chart below the scale pattern shows the location of the roots on the sixth string. The fret placement of the root determines the letter name of the scale. For example, to play the G minor pentatonic scale, position the pattern so the first finger is on the third fret, sixth string (G). Practice playing the G minor pentatonic scale starting with the first finger on the sixth string, third fret. Play the notes one at a time beginning with the sixth string, first finger, followed by the sixth string fourth finger. Then, move to the fifth string - first finger - and progress to the first string. Practice this scale pattern beginning the several different frets. Practice playing this scale from low notes to high and vice versa.

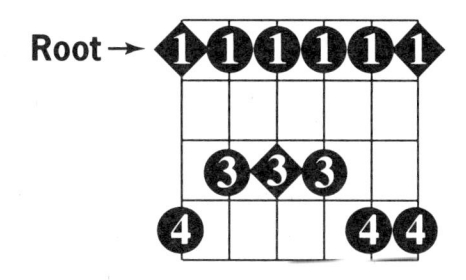

Fret	1	3	5	7	8	10	12
Root Name	F	G	A	B	C	D	E

To sharp the scale, move the pattern up one fret. For example, G♯ minor pentatonic scale begins in the fourth fret. To flat the scale, move it down one fret. For example, B♭ minor pentatonic begins in the sixth fret.

The scale pattern drawn below is the same minor pentatonic scale with the root on the sixth string. However, two circled numbers have been added. The addition of the circled **2** and **4** on strings five and three turns the minor pentatonic scale into a blues scale.

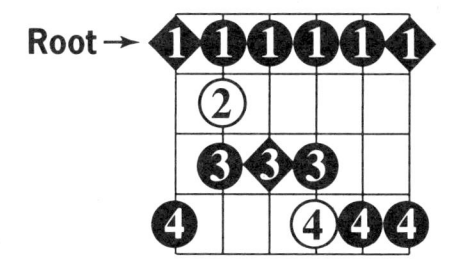

The following blues solo is in the key of A and uses the notes from the moveable minor pentatonic scale beginning on the sixth string, fifth fret (A). Remember, when a number is on top of another number, play the two strings at the same time.

Summer Blues, Summer Not

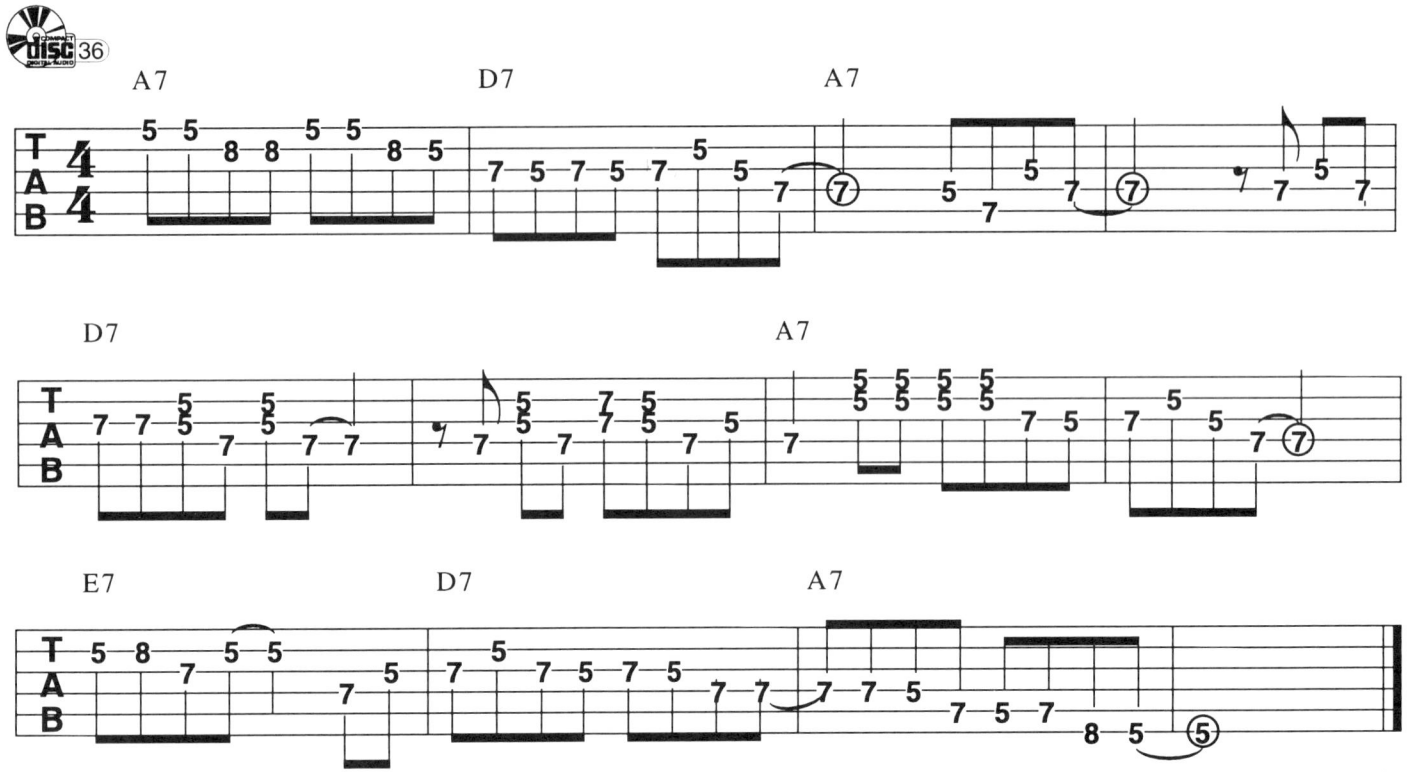

When improvising over the blues progression, any of the notes from the minor pentatonic scale can be used in the solo. The notes must come from the minor pentatonic scale which has the same letter name as the key. Even when the chords in the progression change, the notes used for the solo can come from the scale of the key. For example, when creating an improvised blues solo in the key of A, the notes used in the solo can come from the A minor pentatonic scale. Wether the chords are A7, D7, or E7, the A minor pentatonic scale can be used to play the solo because the entire progression is in the key of A.

Practice creating your own improvised solo to the progression at the top of this page and the blues in other keys by using the notes from the moveable minor pentatonic scale.

The pattern for the moveable minor pentatonic scale with the root on the fifth string is drawn below. The addition of the circled numbers will convert the minor pentatonic scale into the blues scale. Like the moveable scale pattern with the root of the sixth string, this pattern may be moved up and down the neck. Again, the letter name of the root will determine the letter name of the scale. The chart for the location of the roots on the fifth string is drawn below the scale pattern. Practice this scale pattern with, and without, the circled numbers ② & ④.

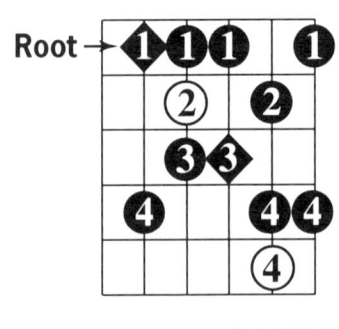

Fret	2	3	5	7	8	10	12
Root Name	B	C	D	E	F	G	A

Practice playing the following blues solo in the key of D. All of the notes used in the solo come from the D minor pentatonic scale with the root on the fifth string, fifth fret (D). Notice this solo is 24 measures long. The 12-bar blues form is played twice.

I Know What You Mean

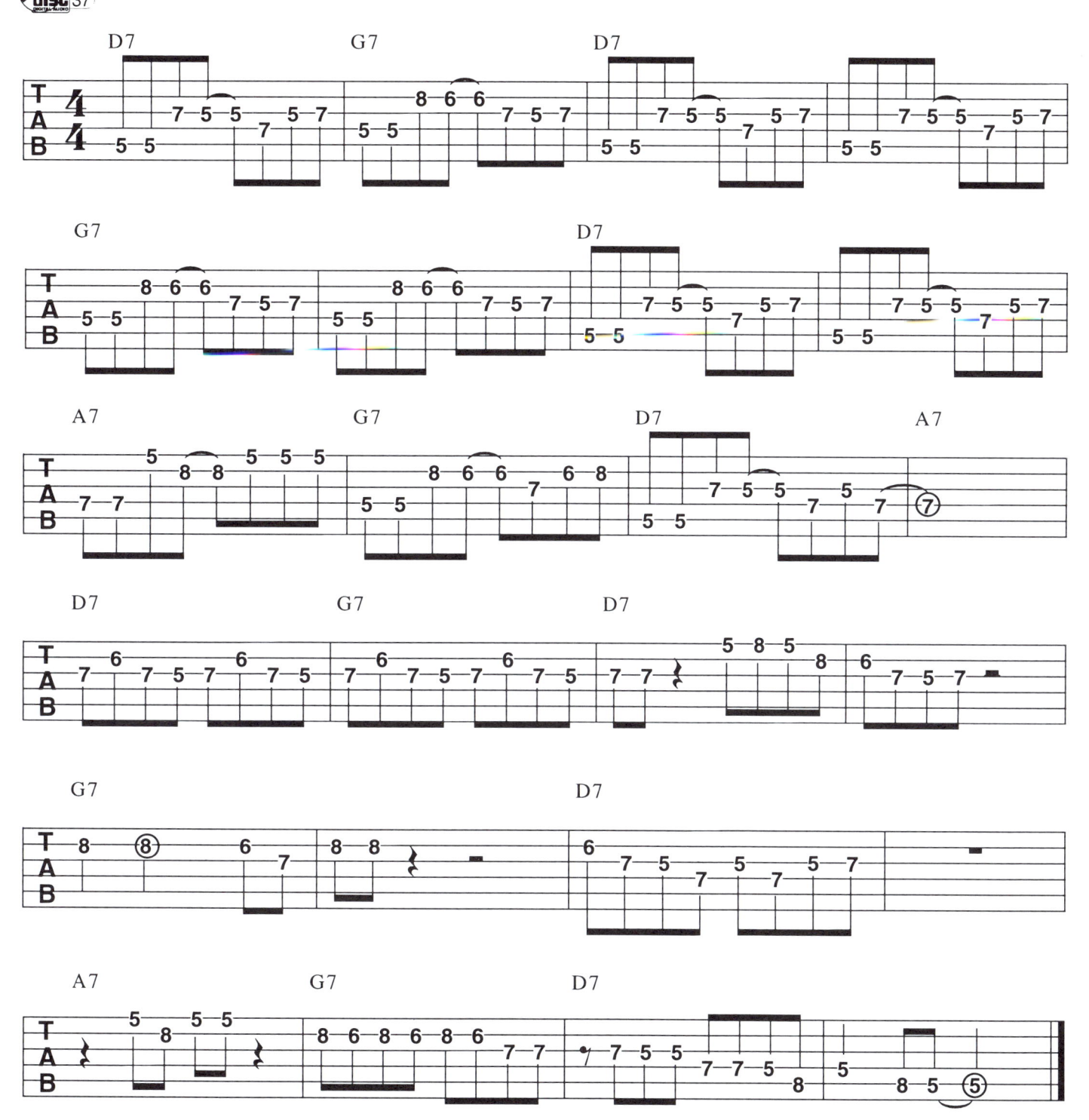

Writing Blues Lyrics

Writing lyrics to a blues song can be very simple. All that is required is to rhyme one word. The common blues progression is 12 measures (12 bars) long. This 12-measure progression can be divided into three groups of four measures. Each group of four measures is called a **phrase**. Phrases are separated by pauses in the melody.

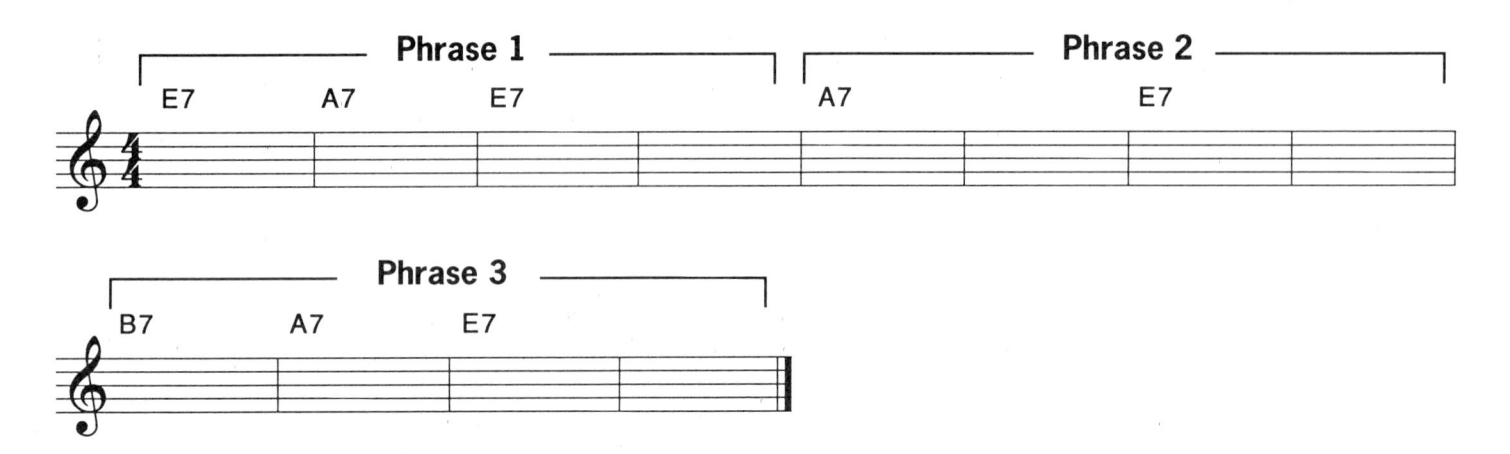

After each phrase there is usually a pause. Within each phrase, one or two sentences of lyrics can be written. For example:

Blues in the morn-in', I get the blues at night.

In the blues, it is very common for the lyrics and the melody in the second phrase to be the same as the lyrics and melody in the first phrase.

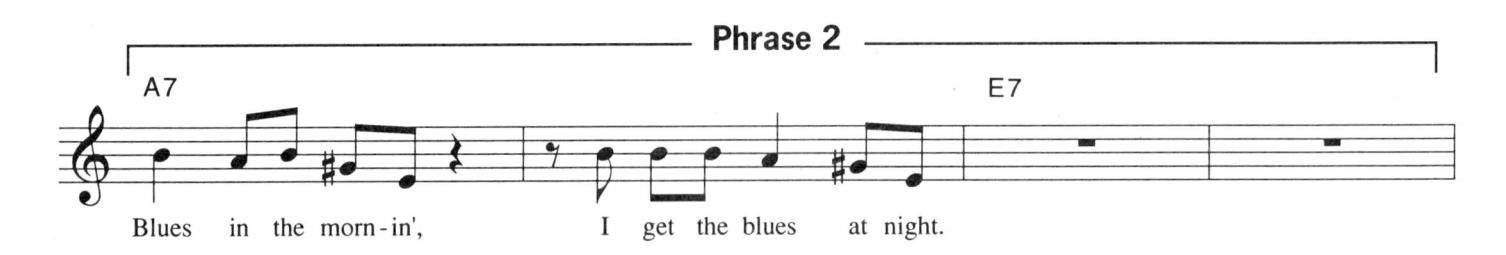

Blues in the morn-in', I get the blues at night.

In the third phrase the lyrics and the melody usually change and the last word of the third phrase rhymes with the last word in phrases 1 and 2.

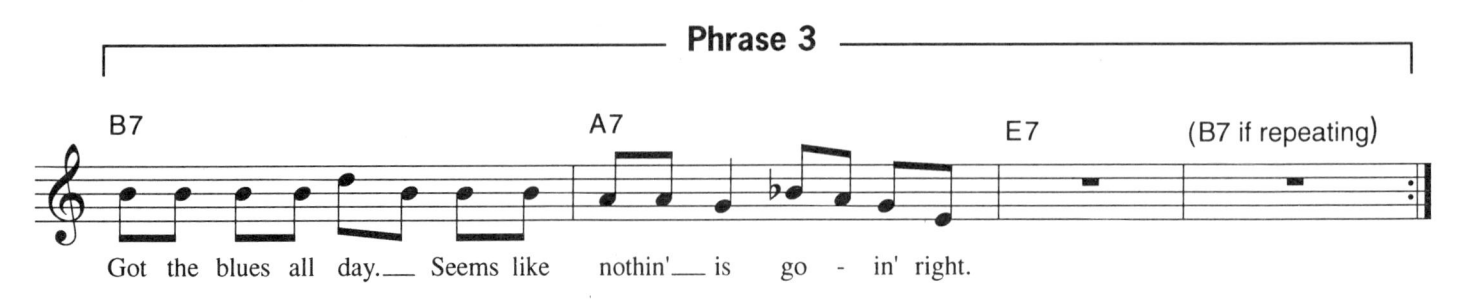

Got the blues all day. Seems like nothin' is go-in' right.

Written below is a 12-bar blues melody. Write in your own lyrics under the notes. You may have to modify the rhythm of the melody slighly to fit your words.

Writing Your Own Blues Song

Write your own lyrics to this blues melody.

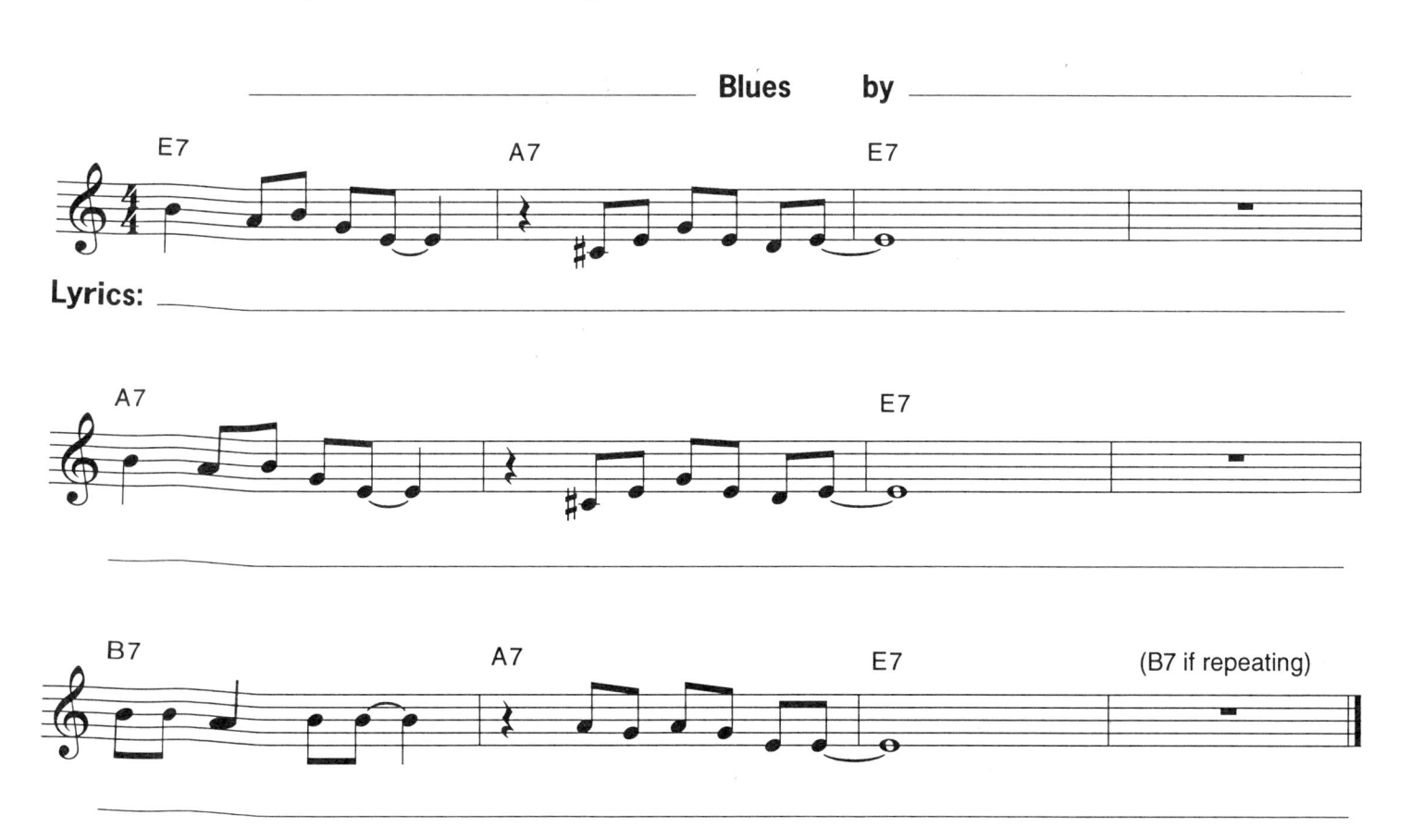

_____ Blues   by _____

Lyrics: _____

Common Chords

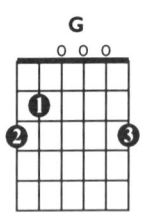

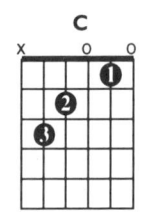

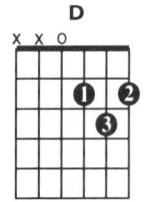

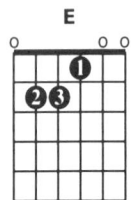

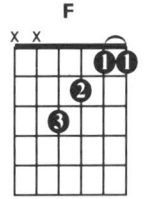

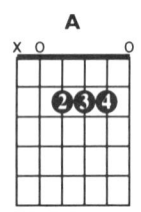

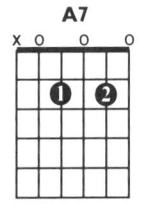

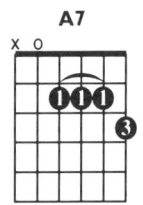

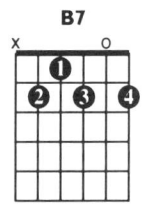

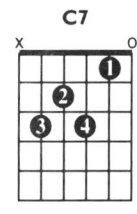

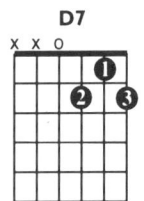

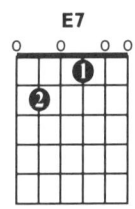

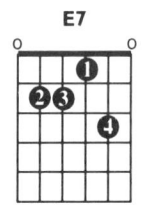

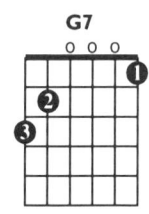

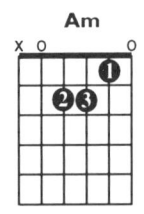

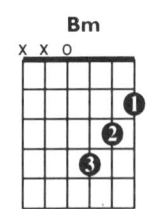

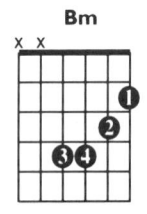

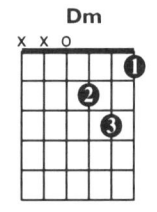

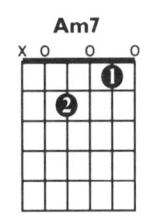

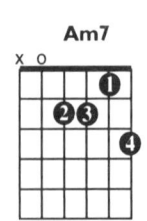

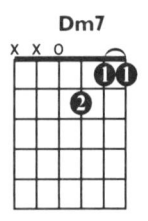

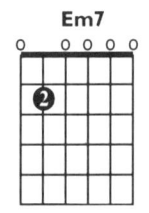

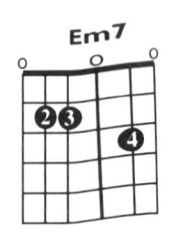